YORK NOTES

General Editors: Professor A.N. Jeffares (*University of Stirling*) & Professor Suheil Bushrui (*American University of Beirut*) out of print.

John Betjeman

SELECTED POEMS

Notes by Harry Blamires

MA (OXFORD)
Former Head of the English Department,
King Alfred's College, Winchester

LONGMAN
YORK PRESS

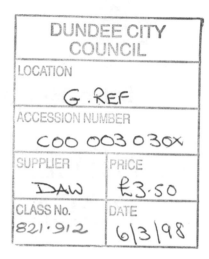
YORK PRESS
Immeuble Esseily, Place Riad Solh, Beirut.

LONGMAN GROUP UK LIMITED
Longman House, Burnt Mill, Harlow,
Essex CM20 2JE, England
Associated companies, branches and representatives
throughout the world

First published in 1992

ISBN 0-582-09643-X

Phototypeset by Gem Graphics, Trenance, Mawgan Porth, Cornwall
Printed in Hong Kong
WC/01

Contents

Part 1
_____

Introduction

The life of John Betjeman

John Betjeman was born in Highgate, London, in 1906. His father, Ernest Betjemann, carried on the family cabinet-making business which John's grandfather had made prosperous by inventing what was called the 'Tantalus'. It was a kind of cage in which decanters could be locked to prevent servants from helping themselves to wine and spirits. The family was of Dutch or German origin, and though John's great-grandfather had spelt his name 'Betjeman', his grandfather and father reverted to the form 'Betjemann'. During the First World War John's mother felt it desirable to drop the Germanic final 'n'. Ernest and his wife were not a very happily married couple and they quarrelled a good deal. John was their only child to survive.

Soon after John's birth the family moved from Parliament Hill Mansions to 31 West Hill, Highgate, a villa in a much more respectable district socially. John was first sent to school at Byron House, and a little girl who was his contemporary there has since recalled how he once announced that he was going to be a poet when he grew up. At his next school, Highgate Junior School, he had an experience of bullying. However, the poet T. S. Eliot (1888–1965) was briefly a master there and John presented him with a manuscript of poems, *The Best of Betjeman*. From there John was sent as a boarder to the Dragon School, Oxford, a school where sufficient freedom was allowed to the pupils for John to be able to cycle around the city and neighbouring villages and to begin to develop his life-long interest in church architecture. While John was at the Dragon School, his parents moved to a house in Church Street, Chelsea, and from there, during the holidays, John began to explore London.

It was Ernest Betjeman's habit to take his family on annual trips to Cornwall. At first they stayed in a boarding house at Trebetherick on the north coast near Padstow, and eventually Ernest Betjeman built a house there called 'Undertown'. John early grew to love the place. He made friends with the children of other well-to-do families who chose to have second homes or to spend their holidays there. One of the features of the poet's early life was the wide range of people he encountered through the different worlds of the London home, the boarding school, the Cornish holidays, and his father's business and sporting connections.

In 1920 John was sent to Marlborough College, Wiltshire, a public school which at the time seems to have incorporated most of the worst aspects of the system. There was organised bullying on a brutal scale. The hearties and athletes among the boys terrorised the rest. Young Betjeman began defensively to cultivate the role of eccentric. He contributed to a magazine called 'The Heretick', which was designed to counter the ascendancy of the philistines in the school. Among his friends at Marlborough was the future poet Louis MacNeice (1907–63).

Betjeman went up to Magdalen College, Oxford, in 1925. Oxford life fascinated him. He had now acquired a group of intellectual interests, poetry and church architecture especially, and he was a devout Anglo-Catholic with an enthusiasm for the colourful ritual which marked the Anglo-Catholic revival of the inter-war years. He associated both with the aesthetes and with the aristocrats. He had been repelled by the bourgeois world his father and mother inhabited. The fact that Ernest Betjeman had been, from the first, anxious for his son to succeed him in the family business became a source of dissension. Ernest Betjeman was a well-meaning father and John was his only son. John's Oxford career made a mockery of all his father's hopes and ambitions. He threw away money on clothes, became a regular attender at expensive lunch parties, and was taken up by friends whose means were far beyond his own. Moreover he did little work. He cut tutorials. He made absurd gestures, once telling his tutor C. S. Lewis (1898–1963) that Lord Alfred Douglas (1870–1945) was a better poet than Shakespeare. He exasperated Lewis by idleness and dilettantism. He snapped his fingers at authority in a variety of ways. He repeatedly failed a compulsory examination in Divinity and was eventually sent down.

His first job after this setback was as a schoolmaster at a preparatory school at Gerrard's Cross, but in 1931 he was given a post on *The Architectural Review*. He had begun to write stories and poems for magazines and, helped by a wealthy Oxford friend, he published his first book of poems *Mount Zion* (1931). The book softened his father's attitude, and he said that he hoped John's royalties would soon match those of the popular playwright Noel Coward (1899–1973).

Betjeman maintained his upper-class connections and he fell in love with Penelope Chetwode. Her father, Field-Marshal Lord Chetwode, was Commander-in-Chief of the British Army in India. He and Lady Chetwode were on visiting terms with the King and Queen. They sometimes stayed with the royal family for the week-end, and they took a dim view of Betjeman as a future son-in-law. Nevertheless the couple were married in 1933 and had two children, Paul and Camilla. The same year saw the publication of *Ghastly Good Taste*, with its sub-title, 'a depressing story of the Rise and Fall of English Architecture'. The young couple lived for a short time in London, then, in 1934, moved to a country farmhouse at

Uffington, Berkshire. Betjeman commuted to London, for he was made film critic of the *London Evening Standard* in 1935. Indeed he was a prolific journalist in the 1930s, contributing book reviews and architectural pieces to various periodicals. *Continual Dew*, a second volume of poems, appeared in 1937.

When war broke out in 1939 Betjeman first had a post in the Ministry of Information, and then, in 1941, was sent as UK Press Attaché to Dublin. He was so successful in his public relations there that, when he returned to England in 1943, he received great praise in the Irish press and a signed photograph from President de Valera. Back home, after another spell at the Ministry of Information, he was transferred in 1944 to the Admiralty at Bath. The war over, the Betjemans moved into a country house at Farnborough in 1945. From there, in 1951, they moved to Wantage, where Penelope ran a waterfowl farm and a teashop called 'King Alfred's Kitchen'.

During the war Betjeman had become widely known for his performances on 'The Brains Trust', one of the BBC's most successful radio programmes. His work as writer and broadcaster drew him away from the country life that Penelope loved. A new barrier came between them in 1948 when Penelope became a Roman Catholic. Betjeman himself firmly resisted pressure from the novelist Evelyn Waugh (1903–66) for him to leave the Church of England, and Penelope's conversion must have been painful to him. She had her own interests as a keen horsewoman and a student of India. She published travel books under her maiden name. Although there was no quarrel, their lives drifted apart. Betjeman acquired a house in Cloth Fair in the City of London. It was a house, he claimed, from which 'everything could be reached on foot, down alleys and passages'.

The 1950s proved a most productive decade for Betjeman. His volume *A Few Late Chrysanthemums* (1954) was followed in 1958 by *Collected Poems*, which was a runaway success. Thereafter he was established as a public figure by his appearances on the television screen. He led viewers on guided tours of buildings and cities. His infectious enthusiasm, his sense of humour, and his utter freedom from pedantry made him an entertaining performer on the screen. He wanted others to share the great pleasures of the eye that he enjoyed, 'to make people look at things that are beautiful, particularly buildings', he said.

His later publications in verse included his autobiographical poem *Summoned by Bells* (1960), *High and Low* (1966), and *A Nip in the Air* (1974). He was knighted in 1969, and when C. Day Lewis (1904–72) died, Betjeman succeeded him as Poet Laureate. By this time he was beginning to suffer from Parkinson's Disease. In 1983 he publicly named a British Rail engine 'Sir John Betjeman' from a wheelchair. He died in 1984 at Trebetherick.

Historical and cultural background

The span of Betjeman's lifetime, from 1906 to 1984, covered a period of momentous change in the physical and social environment of the United Kingdom. Betjeman was a person acutely sensitive to the physical environment. He was also, as he grew older, one for whom the impressions of childhood and youth had indelibly marked his tastes and seated long-lasting affections in his emotional make-up. For any of us, the world as it was when we were children is idealised in our recollections, and it becomes a reference point by which we pass judgment on the later developments around us.

Developments during Betjeman's lifetime turned him into a stern critic of modern life and stirred his nostalgia for the past. There was a rapid increase in population which caused cities, and London especially, to spread the carpet of urban industry and suburban housing over miles and miles of previously attractive countryside. It is ironical that the spreading suburbia which Betjeman so much regretted was largely caused by desirable developments in municipal and private housing, which ameliorated the squalid and congested conditions in overcrowded city slums. What Betjeman experienced in his childhood was not the life of the slum-dweller but the physically comfortable life of the middle class. The family home in Highgate was a stucco villa suitable for a modestly well-to-do family able to afford to keep a brougham and employ servants. People in such circumstances naturally did not relish the encroachment of creeping urbanisation.

Betjeman was to live through two world wars. A feature of such wars is that civilisation tends to stand still during hostilities. The England of 1919 was not very different in appearance to the eye to the England of 1914. But after the hostilities, changes rocketed forward. The 1920s and 1930s, the period of Betjeman's young manhood, transformed the physical, social, and psychological environment of the country. The Victorian and Edwardian ages had been the great days of the railways. When Betjeman's family went to Cornwall, they did so at first by train. When the little boy was taken shopping in Kentish Town, he travelled by tram. The extent to which the internal combustion engine has transformed the environment of our country is now a popular cause of worry. Not that the full menace of the automobile was evident from the start. Betjeman came to lament the damage it did, but when he celebrated in verse the excursions his father's workers made by a charabanc in 'Essex', he made no complaint about the mode of transport. When he recalled the shooting trip he made with his father in 'Hertfordshire' and the 'slow drive home by motor car', he perhaps hit the nail on the head. In the early days of motoring driving was comparatively slow and vehicles on the roads were scarce. Excessive speeds, cluttered roads, and miles of static traffic came most damagingly only after the Second World War.

While the municipal housing estates were going up in the 1920s and petrol cars and buses were beginning to throng the streets of London, there were areas of life less subject to change. Life at Oxford, when Betjeman went up in 1925, had not changed much from pre-war days. By far the majority of students were there because their parents could afford to pay all their fees and expenses. The number of those wholly dependent upon scholarships was comparatively minute. The vast majority of students were educated at public schools, and a fair number were members of the aristocracy. Since in so many cases academic promise had not brought them there and academic motivation was lacking, there were many who took lightly the studies which were supposed to be the main business of the place.

The life of the Oxford student was the life of a gentleman. The tutorial system required attendance once a week with the tutor, but whether students attended any of the lectures provided was up to them. There were students who went out riding, students who gave themselves to athletics, and students who made life a round of sherry parties, luncheons, and dinners. The pattern of life had its roots in Edwardian England. A student would have his own sitting-room with bedroom attached. A servant ('scout') would be at his disposal: to light his coal fire in the morning, to bring up to his room the breakfast he ordered, and to bring his lunch and tea there as requested. If a student invited a guest or guests to any of these meals, the scout would serve whatever number of meals was required. This was the way middle-class people lived in Edwardian days and it lasted in Oxford up to the start of the Second World War. The public schools sent both their hearties and their contemporary opponents, the aesthetes, to Oxbridge. A student might choose to join the one group or the other. Among the friends Betjeman made at Oxford was the artist Osbert Lancaster (1908–86). He also made aristocratic friendships which resulted in his being invited to stay at country houses both in England and in Ireland. He took part in dramatic performances, he edited the magazine *Cherwell*, he made friends with W. H. Auden (1907–73) at Christ Church, and maintained his connection with Louis MacNeice. He dined out, he invented a cocktail, he ran up bills for books at Blackwells; he also practised his religion, becoming a regular worshipper at Pusey House where full ritual was maintained for the Sunday High Mass.

While the extravagance of Betjeman's way of life among the aesthetes and the aristocrats made him very much a young man of his age, he seems to have been quite untouched by the literary avant-garde. He never fitted neatly into predicted categories. He revelled with hedonists but was faithful at church attendance. He frolicked with bright young things, but the poetic movement of the day did not interest him. T. S. Eliot and

Ezra Pound (1885–1972) had begun to dominate the poetic scene for the cognoscenti. *Ulysses* by James Joyce (1882–1941) was published in 1922. The Sitwells were the rage of the 1920s after Edith Sitwell (1887–1964) produced *Façade* in 1922. There was a great deal of experimentation with so-called free verse. Yet, from the first, Betjeman concentrated on traditional metres and patterned stanza forms. Moreover, there was also a great deal of experimentation in using varied imagery in associative sequences which by-passed the need for clear logical or narrative progress. Yet Betjeman concentrated on clarity and directness of utterance. The surface meaning was always susceptible to immediate reception.

As a poet, Betjeman ignored the modern movement. He went rather for inspiration to his Victorian predecessors. He borrowed their rhythmic patterns and stanza forms; he echoed their phrases and cadences. It was not just Tennyson (1809–92), Meredith (1828–1909), Swinburne (1837–1909), Housman (1859–1936), Longfellow (1807–82), and Newbolt (1862–1938) from whom he learned, but also forgotten minor Victorian poets, and the writers whose verses make up the popular hymns in *Hymns Ancient and Modern*. The simplicity and directness of his language put him in place in a line of English poets who stand out clearly against the background of twentieth-century experimentation. It includes Thomas Hardy (1840–1928), Edward Thomas (1878–1917), W. H. Auden, and Philip Larkin (1914–85). Both Auden and Larkin have championed his work. The poetic tradition these writers belong to eschews obscurity and the kind of congestion in texture which marks the poetry of, say, Dylan Thomas (1914–53). Built-in grandeur, cosmopolitan allusiveness, mythic resonance, and all manner of pretentiousness were alien to these poets. After decades in which obscurity has flourished, changing taste has now brought poets such as Betjeman fully back in fashion.

Just as Betjeman's poetry has helped to renew the taste for simplicity and directness in verse, so too his championing of Victorian architecture and Victorian artefacts, which seemed so wildly perverse in his younger days, has now helped firmly to establish a change in public taste. The renewal of the Victorian style has rescued us from the architectural horrors of the 1960s in some of our shopping precincts and our pedestrianised city centres.

Betjeman's self-portrait

Wordsworth (1770–1850) wrote a long study of his own poetic development in blank verse, *The Prelude* (1850). Betjeman decided to do the same and wrote *Summoned by Bells* (1960) also in blank verse. It may not represent Betjeman the poet at his best, but the frank account of how he came to poethood is certainly a helpful guide to the reader in taking stock of his work. It is written in nine 'Chapters'.

CHAPTER I **'Before MCMXIV'**

This covers the years of Betjeman's childhood up to 1914. Betjeman recaptures his earliest impressions of life at West Hill. He recreates the tranquillity and beauty of the area on the periphery of town and country. He records his sense of the family's exact social position between the wealthy and the less affluent. What early ministers to his sense of insecurity is the family concern about their German-sounding name in the approach to the First World War and his introduction to the dingier environment of nearby Kentish Town. What ministers to his sense of security is the atmosphere of his own home with its buttered toast and remoteness from the smell of poverty. The house was 'full of maids' and a 'hateful nurse' Maud who punished him cruelly. His great refuge was his beloved teddy-bear Archibald.

CHAPTER II **'The Dawn of Guilt'**

Betjeman describes his early fond relationship with his father, and his father's doomed attempts to interest him in the family firm. He gives a vivid picture of the craftsmen at work in cabinet-making, silver-plating, and polishing, and of his own failure to feel deeply interested in the ultimate purpose of it all. He finds beauty in the Cornish scenery rather than in the products of his father's firm. A sense of guilt derives not only from the disappointment in failing all his father's ambitions for him, but also from his feeling that he is letting down the employees. But he has decided to become a poet and frankly prints specimens of his earliest attempts at verse.

CHAPTER III **'Highgate'**

Betjeman tells how he first fell in love with Peggy Purey-Cust, the daughter of an Admiral, was once asked to the grand house to tea, but was thereafter kept painfully at a distance. His main unhappiness at Byron House, which he found a 'happy school', was fear of two boys who ill-treated him. Sadly they followed him to be a continuing nuisance at his next school, Highgate Junior School. There his interest in poetry was touched by Poe's 'The Bells', Longfellow's 'The Wreck of the *Hesperus*', and Campbell's 'The Soldier's Dream', all stock works in school poetry books of the time.

CHAPTER IV **'Cornwall in Childhood'**

This section gives a lyrical account of the family holidays in Cornwall, recapturing all the childhood delight in the train journey and the return to the beloved sea-shore. The happiness is palpable in Betjeman's account of his adventures with other boys and girls. The vivid recollection of sounds and smells and sights shows how early there developed in Betjeman that sensitivity to the detail of the environment, natural and human, which was to serve him so well as a poet.

CHAPTER V 'Private School'

This section covers Betjeman's life at the Dragon School. He reveals his growing ingenuity when he gets out of a fight he has been challenged to by pretending to have received sudden news of his mother's grave illness. The outer world impinges when the headmaster announces news of former pupils killed on the Western Front and the boys stick flags on maps along the River Somme. But the main interest here is Betjeman's account of how he cycled around Oxford and the neighbourhood, becoming an enthusiastic explorer of church architecture.

CHAPTER VI 'London'

Betjeman returns from the Dragon School at the end of term to find that his parents have moved to Chelsea. This represents a further rise in the social scale, but he sadly misses the familiar surroundings of 'happy Highgate'. His one consolation is that a school friend lives near by. Together they spend whole days exploring every line on the Underground railway. Second-hand bookshops are another enthusiasm; and Betjeman explains carefully how steel engravings in old books took him out of his own period mentally into the early nineteenth-century days of stage coaches and street cries. On Sundays it is a special delight to respond to the call of church bells in out-of-the-way corners of London and be present at Evensong.

CHAPTER VII 'Marlborough'

Betjeman shakes off any restraint in describing the barbarities of life at Marlborough, where the worst nineteenth-century traditions of public-school practice made for the tedium of absurdly austere routines, and for the maximum misery at the hands of bullies among the boys and unimaginative pedants among the staff.

CHAPTER VIII 'Cornwall in Adolescence'

Betjeman reflects on his relationship with his parents. His mother is vividly sketched. We hear her speaking; we enter into her reveries, and what emerges is the portrait of a brave, patient woman, mentally limited, sustaining herself on rather sentimental slogans and equally sentimental novels. Betjeman now feels that he ought to have revealed the real love he had for her. His father is pictured from the outside. He is a grumbler who throws his weight about; yet implicit in his bad temper is grave disappointment with his son. Betjeman here openly rebels against him. He cycles around Cornwall and meets a parish priest who lends him Arthur Machen's *The Secret Glory*. The intention is to wean him from reliance on the externals of religion to a sense of the mystical. Betjeman tries in vain to cultivate such a sense.

CHAPTER IX **'The Opening World'**

Betjeman finds Oxford life pure delight. He relishes the dignity and freedom of having private rooms at Magdalen. He loves lunch parties at 'The George' and High Mass at Pusey House. For himself he finds the supremely 'essential' externals of religious practice effective 'steps to truth'. We see him at Sunday morning gatherings with fellow aesthetes. We see him driving out to Sunday lunch at the great country house of Sezincote near Burton-on-the-Hill. We see him dining at Wadham College with Maurice Bowra (1898–1971), whose lightly-worn learning and freedom from pretentiousness teach him 'far more than all my tutors did'. But the experience of delight melts away as he fails the Divinity examination and is sent down.

A note on the text

John Betjeman's *Collected Poems* was first published in 1958 and was repeatedly reprinted. The poems studied here are all included in the fourth edition of *Collected Poems* published in 1979. The *Collected Poems* arranges the poems in ten sections according to the dates of the earlier volumes in which they appeared. The sections are headed: *Mount Zion* (1932), *Continual Dew* (1937), *Old Lights for New Chancels* (1940), *New Bats in Old Belfries* (1945), *Selected Poems* (1948), *A Few Late Chrysanthemums* (1954), *Poems in the Porch* (1954), *Poems written after 1954*, *High and Low* (1966), and *A Nip in the Air* (1974). The poems selected for treatment here are dealt with in the order in which they appear in *Collected Poems*. An alphabetical index of titles of poems discussed in Part 2 is given on page 79.

Summaries
of SELECTED POEMS

'Death in Leamington'   *Mount Zion*

In simple sentences we hear of an old lady's death. Then Nurse comes in, unaware of what has happened, to unroll the blinds, light the gas, tend the fire, and give the patient her tea. She goes through her familiar routine, and everything is registered in a matter-of-fact tone. Leamington Spa is a town of decaying gentility, and a decaying gentlewoman has died. Death, with all its gravity and finality, is here one more everyday event, like the turning down of the gas.

NOTES AND GLOSSARY:

Leamington Spa:	once a fashionable watering place, it has impressive terraces of Regency and Victorian architecture, attractive parks and gardens, and an air of faded gentility
Breast high:	see Thomas Hood's (1799–1845) 'Ruth' – 'She stood breast high amid the corn'
Chintzy:	chintz, the highly coloured printed fabric used for curtains and furniture covers became especially associated with well-to-do 'cottagy' interiors
stucco:	the decorative plaster-work on walls

'Croydon'   *Mount Zion*

In spite of the title the subject is really 'Uncle Dick'. He is not given a specific character: he was young once and now he is dead, and that is almost all there is about it. What gives the poem its emotional quality is the way this summary of a human story is localised. Uncle Dick was born in such and such a house, he walked daily to school at Whitgift, and explored Coulsdon woods with his friends. Plenty of Victorian verse treated death as a facile source of sentiment. The contrast between the delights of boyhood and the fact of mortality could readily be pushed home in verse to tearful effect. But Betjeman makes no use of the ready-made machinery of pathos. The simple recital of events has a touching authenticity. Repeated use of the phrase 'Your Uncle Dick' turns the poet into one who is not speaking directly to the reader, but recording and dwelling on what he has been told. The reader is drawn to his side in taking the facts in.

NOTES AND GLOSSARY:
Whitgift: a well-known grammar school at Croydon
Coulsdon woodlands: Croydon was still surrounded by countryside when Dick was young
spadgers: a dialect word for 'sparrows'

'The Arrest of Oscar Wilde at the Cadogan Hotel' *Continual Dew*

Oscar Wilde (1854–1900) lost a libel case brought against the Marquis of Queensberry in 1895 for accusing him of sodomy. It was then plain that Wilde himself would have to be prosecuted on a charge of homosexual practices. By holding their hands for a time the authorities did what they could to allow Wilde to get away from the country and escape prosecution. But Wilde, seemingly through a mixture of lethargy and obstinacy, simply sat around in his hotel, virtually waiting for the law to act.

Wilde sits drinking in his hotel bedroom, apparently giving no thought to the situation he is in. Rather he is chattering about trivial things – the latest edition of *The Yellow Book* and the quality of service in the hotel. He calls for clothes to be collected and sent after him as though his next destination were another hotel. He seems to be living in an unreal mental world when the police burst in. Their broad cockney accents grate farcically on the ear. Yet in the last stanza a new note is sounded. It is a staggering and 'terrible-eyed' Wilde who has to brush past the palms on the staircase. Farce turns into tragedy.

By presenting events in terms of mingled absurdity and tragedy, Betjeman no doubt intended to pin-point the paradoxical character of Wilde, the great master of paradox, an artist for whom the distinction between the comic and the serious never properly held good.

NOTES AND GLOSSARY:
bees-winged eyes: Wilde was by this time grossly obese
Robbie: Wilde's friend, Robert Ross (1869–1918)
Yellow Book: a quarterly which was first issued in 1894 and lasted some three years
Approval of what is approved of: a characteristic Wildean witticism. (It is as false to praise what other people are praising as to keep a vow you have made)

'Slough' *Continual Dew*

The poet calls for aircraft to swarm over Slough and destroy it with bombs. It would be a friendly act, for the place is no longer fit for human habitation. The clutter of modern industrialisation, which has replaced grassland and farming, should be obliterated. The tinned foods that service the factory canteens are symbols of a pervasive artificiality: even the air the workers breathe is 'tinned' through the air-conditioning system, and their minds are processed and mass-produced like the food they eat. The poet proclaims that the shoddy new housing estates should be destroyed, and bitterly lambasts the well-fed ('double-chinned') planners and profiteers who are responsible for the mess and the consequent human misery. But he would spare the young clerks, prematurely ageing ('bald') who do their office work. They are occupied in a kind of Hell. Small wonder that they go off to Maidenhead to escape, to chatter in artificial 'ye olde' pubs about sports and cars, oblivious to the real world with stars overhead. Their wives too are busy in covering living humanity with modern artifices, frizzing and dyeing their hair and painting their finger-nails. Let the bombs fall and cleanse the earth for the real life of ploughing and reaping. The land is gasping for it.

NOTES AND GLOSSARY:
Slough provided Betjeman with an apt target in his eagerness to assault the ugliness of twentieth-century urbanism. Last century it was a small market town, but twentieth-century developments transformed it into the largest industrial centre in Berkshire. A government transport depot was sited there during the First World War, and afterwards it was converted into a vast Trading Estate with hundreds of factories – the first such estate in the country. The young Betjeman's political and social radicalism comes out in his blistering attack on the typical capitalist profiteer ('And get that man'). The violence of it puts Betjeman for a moment into line with the left-wing 'poets of the thirties' such as Cecil Day-Lewis. But the dominant theme of the poem is the contrast between reality and artifice, between life in contact with nature and life overlaid with the trappings of industrial technology.

half-a-crown:	twelve and a half contemporary pence; apparently a house could be bought for a deposit of £97 and a mortgage repayment of about £6 per year, but wages were low
Maidenhead:	an ancient Berkshire town beautifully situated on the Thames; it retained its charm and became a London dormitory town

---

'Love in a Valley'   *Continual Dew*

Betjeman frequently makes use of the work of earlier poets. Often he is content to borrow a phrase or a line, or to mimic a rhythmic pattern. Here he models his poem closely on Meredith's 'Love in the Valley'. Meredith's poem is a rapturous celebration of young love, and it is effected in a throbbingly joyous rhythmic pattern. In challenging comparison with

Meredith, Betjeman no doubt took a risk, but his technique served him well.

In Meredith's poem it is the young man who speaks: here it is the young lady. There is a note of innocence and freshness similar to that of Meredith's poem. The young lady longs to be driven by her beloved Lieutenant to their Surrey home in his sports car. She pictures the delights of the journey through the countryside. The feverish rhythm conveys the excitement of increasing anticipation as they approach the house down the drive and finally reach the door. As the couple fling open the curtains and the windows on arrival to see the sunset and hear the passing trains, a new note is sounded. The outburst is not after all a purely joyous anticipation. For the Lieutenant is 'portable'. He can be shifted about the world like an object by wills other than his own. He is to be posted to China, leaving the young lady to 'lonely shopping'. The drive they set out on is a last journey together before separation.

'Dorset'	Continual Dew

The poet obviously delights in rolling out the sonorous names of Dorset villages. They are in themselves evocative of a romantic and peaceful countryside. The poem is built on a dual contrast. The first is the contrast between the daily toil of the locals and their evening leisure activities. The men who have ploughed the fields in the morning hold playing-cards in the evening as they gather for whist drives in their social centres. The hands of the farmers' wives, which milked the cows on Sunday morning, are gloved as they hold their hymn-books in church in the evening. The last stanza pictures the scene inside the church for evensong. The smelly oil-lamps light up the pitch-pine pews. But the contrast between farming and socialising or worshipping is submerged under a deeper contrast in the last line of each stanza. It is the contrast between the life now lived in field or club or church and the fact of death. The churchyard contains the bodies of those who once lived: and Betjeman gives the contrast a keen cutting-edge by listing, among the dead, men and women who were very much alive when the poem was written.

NOTES AND GLOSSARY:
Dorset was Thomas Hardy's county. Hardy wrote a celebrated poem called 'Friends Beyond' which begins: 'William Dewy, Tranter Reuben, Farmer Ludlow late at plough,/Robert's kin, and John's, and Ned's/And the Squire, and Lady Susan, lie in Mellstock churchyard now.' Mellstock is the fictional village of Hardy's novel *Under the Greenwood Tree* (1872). It represents the village of Stinsford where Hardy's own heart was buried. Some of the persons named in Hardy's poem are characters in the novel. Betjeman's adaptation of these lines has a powerful irony. By listing the

names of living celebrities and even some of his old acquaintances alongside the rest, he blends fiction and reality, history and contemporaneity together. None can escape the threat of mortality. Another powerful imaginative touch is the contrast between the eternal light of heaven ('Salem', the new Jerusalem) and the smelly lamps in the church. Betjeman's placing of the word 'waiting' in the last stanza is an ingenious stroke. Centrally emphatic, it sheds on the whole human scene an air of tentativeness and impermanence. The worshippers are waiting for death and for Heaven as well as for the service to begin.

T. S. Eliot: a controversial figure in the 1930s for his innovatory poetic style

H. G. Wells: the novelist (1866–1946), often in the news in the 1930s for his outspoken social radicalism

Edith Sitwell: the poet, a sensational figure in the press after the production of *Façade* (1922), jazzed-up verses declaimed against a musical background by William Walton

Mary Borden: a popular novelist (1886–1968)

Brian Howard: one of Betjeman's contemporaries at Oxford

Harold Acton: an aesthete at Oxford in the 1920s (*b.* 1904)

Light's abode, celestial Salem: the opening words of a popular hymn extolling the joys of Heaven

Gordon Selfridge: businessman (1858–1947), owner of the Oxford Street department store

Edna Best: a well-known film actress (1900–74)

'Exeter' *Continual Dew*

This poem presents a little human story such as might attach to any cathedral city. We see the wife of a local doctor reading in her garden in the sunshine, the book before her flecked with shadows, and the cathedral bells audible from over the garden wall. The book is by Aldous Huxley (1894–1963), novelist and thinker, whose works were avidly devoured in the 1930s by readers with intellectual pretensions, because he was a knowing satirist of the contemporary intelligentsia and he affected a philosophical stance. He was the kind of writer to make people feel that they were in the swim intellectually. So perhaps the lady's desire to be in with the trends of the time explains why her frequent attendance at cathedral services is now a thing of the past. The doctor, her husband, goes driving off without any concern for others. Turning into the main road, he collides with a tram-car and is killed. His body is brought home and laid on the table which used to hold glossy magazines. And under the shock of her bereavement the doctor's wife resumes her former practice of regular worship in the cathedral.

NOTES AND GLOSSARY:
We see Betjeman's verbal subtlety at work in the last line of the first stanza, where the antiquarian flavour of the word 'writ' and the old-world artifice of marking the pronunciation of 'Huxléy' to bring out the rhyme ('HuxLEE') together suggest exactly the rather precious character of the lady's self-conscious intellectual aspirations. Betjeman does not actually spell out the full implications of his lines, but leaves it to the reader to use some imagination. And it appears that, in the days when she was a regular worshipper, she left magazines about the house to catch the eyes of visiting canons' wives, and they were journals that suggested a familiarity with the fashionable social scene. A. Huxley has weaned her taste since then.

Wulfric's altar: St Wulfric was a twelfth-century West-country hermit of great sanctity

riddel posts: the side-posts of the altar which support the curtains surrounding the table

Stanford in A: the musical content of a cathedral service, apart from hymns and psalms, includes settings of the canticles, creeds, and other pieces from the liturgy. Among the Victorian composers who left highly tuneful settings for this purpose was Sir Charles Stanford (1852–1924), and the setting in A major was among the most popular

Colleton Crescent: one of a group of streets between the cathedral close and the river

***The Tatler, The Sketch*, and *The Bystander*:** magazines portraying high society life, in two of which at least Betjeman once figured

---

'Death of King George V'   *Continual Dew*

This poem illustrates how different were Betjeman's public attitudes from those of his Victorian predecessors. In Victorian England verse written to celebrate the deaths of the great (such as Tennyson's elegy on the Duke of Wellington) strove to accumulate loftily grave reflections in sonorous ceremonial idiom. Instead of making any ritual gestures, Betjeman here focuses on George V's true personality. The king had simple tastes. He was fond of shooting and he collected stamps. Betjeman pictures the spirits of the game-birds the king has shot bearing him away up into the Norfolk sky, while his stamp-collection lies neglected at Sandringham, his Norfolk home.

Something of the simplicity of the king's character is suggested by the 'big blue eyes'. What delighted those eyes was the Norfolk countryside he loved to ride over; what offended them was the sight of people wearing the wrong clothes for the occasion. The society he presided over is represented by old men cocooned in well-carpeted country houses, who were honest, decent, simple Christians, and kept up a modest level of churchmanship, going to Holy Communion once a month. This generation stares (in some astonishment, it is implied) at what is to replace the age George V represented. For journalists have photographed Edward VIII arriving back in London by air and not even wearing a hat.

NOTES AND GLOSSARY:
The 'new suburb' represents the new age. Edward VIII's hatlessness contrasts with his father's dislike of the 'wrong clothing'. Perhaps no external feature more vividly represented the death of one era and the birth of a cruder one that rejected many old proprieties, than the abandonment of hats by the young men of the inter-war years.

'Upper Lambourne'   *Old Lights for New Chancels*

The village of Lambourn in Berkshire lies on the River Lambourn with Upper Lambourn a mile or so to the north. (Betjeman's spelling 'Lambourne' appears to be an error.) The valley lies between downs that are used for exercising horses, and Lambourn is celebrated for its racing stables. Apparently it is autumn. As a breeze sends thousands of leaves pattering to the ground, the poet watches the sunlight playing on the trees. The branches, and even the nettles, sway lightly in the breeze, so that patches of sun and shade shift about, and eventually a gleam of light is focused on the headstone of a grave. It marks the burial place of a famous trainer who died in 1923.

A string of horses moves out towards the downs for exercise, and the poet broods on the tough lives of the jockeys, a toughness represented by their shining saddle-leather, their leather breeches, and their leathery skin. He has earlier noticed the 'Feathery' appearance of the ash as it loses its leaves in the autumn wind, and the contrast between 'Feathery ash' and 'leathery Lambourne' is pressed home to form an implicit commentary on the transience of things. Horses and jockeys and trainers move not only out of sight but also out of 'mind'. For all their leatheriness, they are swallowed up by the surrounding downland, the earth which will outlive us all.

NOTES AND GLOSSARY:
Carrara: a town in Tuscany, Italy, long famous for its quarries, producing a rare, flawless white marble
Paid the Final Entrance Fee: the expression represents Betjeman in characteristic vein – as a way of saying 'died' it is at once lightly ironic and yet skates over the risk of

being funny by touching so closely on what was personally important to the trainer

sarsen stone: (originally, it seems, 'Saracen's stones') large boulders or blocks of sandstone to be found scattered over the chalk down

---

'Pot Pourri from a Surrey Garden'   *Old Lights for New Chancels*

Betjeman has borrowed the title of a Victorian diary by Mrs C. W. Earle which gave advice on running a home and garden. He assembles images representative of well-to-do Surrey commuterland – the prams, the horse-riding, the discarded cigarette packet, the conifers, and the wrought-iron gates of the house he is to visit. There is a sense of urgency as he gives his face a quick wash in the bird-bath and wonders which path through the grounds to take. Knowing the tastes of the girl he seeks, he chooses the path to the tennis-courts. For Pam is a strong, well-built young woman whom he admires for her sheer physical prowess. Her brother may play for Woking, but he wouldn't be able to stand up to Pam's backhand drive. She has large, powerful limbs, and as she swipes a ball mistakenly into the rhododendron bushes, she flings back her head in angry arrogance. From this scene the poet shifts his gaze to what he dreams of – a day when the local church bells will ring out for their wedding, and he will be legally entitled to the grand delight of her embrace.

NOTES AND GLOSSARY:
Betjeman's poems expressing devotion to a muscular woman have a comic aspect caused by his way of upsetting some of the accepted conventions of love poetry. Phrases such as 'you great big mountainous sports girl' and 'full of the strength of five' do not represent the familiar currency of love poetry. The hint of arrogance and petulance in the chosen one is also novel in amorous adoration.

Weights: a brand of cigarettes
Malvernian: the brother is an old boy of Malvern School
Hendren: Patsy Hendren was a celebrated cricketer
Windlesham: a village near Bagshot
Butterfield aisle: the architect William Butterfield (1814–1900) was a leader of the 'Gothic Revival' and was involved in the restoration of churches and other old buildings

---

'Trebetherick'   *Old Lights for New Chancels*

Trebetherick is the seaside village in Padstow Bay on the north coast of Cornwall, where Betjeman's parents spent their summer holidays and built a house. This is a poem of childhood memories. Betjeman conjures up vivid images that register the outer scene with brilliant clarity, and at the same time are infused with a range of childhood emotions from delight and excitement to terror and awe. The opening stanza, with its unforgettable image of the yellow flakes of foam trembling like sponges, is alive too with the unromantic realities of seaside picnicking: fleas and sodden bathing costumes, sand in the sandwiches and wasps in the tea. In the second stanza the focus shifts to the wood in the distance, cool and still in summer maybe, but the home of ancient darkness and the place where pheasants and rabbits are butchered by foxes. In the third and fourth stanzas, Betjeman recalls the thrills of storm and blizzard, in which he and his companions waited excitedly for bits of wreckage to be swept up by the tide, and, venturing round the shore, would be hurled against each other by the violence of wind and wave.

NOTES AND GLOSSARY:
As a poem of childhood, this is packed with tumbling impressions of boyhood's physical experiences, all of which are threaded through with acute emotional responses. These are not painstakingly described; they simply 'come through' the scatter of images, whether it is the thrills of the cliff top, dread of the dark wood and the dead animals, or the tense confederacy of the youngsters outfacing together the onrush of the breakers.

thrift:	a sea-shore plant with pink, white, or purple flowers; the stalks emerge from tufts of leaves
bladder-wrack:	a kind of seaweed which has air-bladders in the fronds
tamarisk:	an evergreen shrub with thin branches and minute leaves
Shilla Mill:	a nearby water-mill made more sinister by the fact that in order to get there the children had to trespass
feathery slate:	the cliff is blackened by the rain, but the thin layers or 'scales' of slate have a seemingly featherlike texture when lightning catches them
Greenaway:	the stretch of beach between Polzeath and Trebetherick Point
St. Enodoc:	the church of St Enodoc, a little Norman building, stands on the golf course
Ralph, Vasey . . .:	all were real children among Betjeman's friends at Trebetherick

---

'On a Portrait of a Deaf Man'   *Old Lights for New Chancels*

The poet pictures his father as he remembers him from boyhood. But each memory of what he was like when he was alive is interrupted by the

realisation of what he is like now as a corpse in the grave. Each replacement of the details of the old living portrait by the gruesome reality of
today reminds us too of our mortality and our future in the cemetery. The
loose-fitting clothes give place to the shroud, the mouthful of potatoes to
the mouthful of London clay, and the wise, smiling eyes are devoured by
maggots. The hands that liked to shake the hands of others are disintegrat-
ing. God, the poet laments, asks for faith in himself, yet his handiwork
seems to be represented by this transformation of what lived into sheer
decay.

NOTES AND GLOSSARY:
The poem is especially moving to readers who are aware of the full story
of Betjeman's relationship with his father. There is a portrait here of
a kindly, well-meaning man with simple aspirations to gentility and
appreciative of middle-class comforts. He is also the father who relished
the countryside and wanted to share its lore with his son. Somehow the
gap in full communication and understanding which Ernest Betjeman's
deafness created becomes sadly symptomatic of all that failed in the
relationship between father and son.
that place . . . on Highgate Hill: Highgate Cemetery
Carrara-covered: covered with marble grave-stones

'Henley-on-Thames'   *New Bats in Old Belfries*

The poet stands on a house-boat on the upper Thames and sees the river
winding away into the distance in what looks like a series of lakes of
ever-decreasing size. Nearer at hand, as the water laps against the side of
the boat and flops back again, the sunlight turns the muddy water an amber
colour and makes the ripples sparkle like gems. Beyond the next curve in
the river, bathers are shouting and diving, making a 'breach' in the surface
of the water that sends ripples floating away towards the town of Henley.
On the bank, roses and geranium-baskets brighten the area where the boats
are hired.
    Betjeman recalls the scene nostalgically and longingly – the boats
breaking the surface of the water into sparkling gems, the tough, hatless
ATS girls rowing through the bridge, and the calls of greeting fading
across the waters as they move away.

NOTES AND GLOSSARY:
Henley is a picturesque town on the Thames. Its Royal Regatta, dating
from 1839 and patronised in its early days by the Prince Consort, has long
been a fashionable highlight of the society season.
    The stanza form here, with its careful mixture of shorter and longer
lines, seems to suggest both the alternate lapping of water this way and

that way around the boats, and the undulating progress of the river itself between the alternately widening and narrowing banks.

reach: the stretch of water between two bends which can be seen in one view

prow-promoted gems: the prow of a boat, breaking the surface of the water, causes the ripples to flash like jewels in the sunshine

ATS: women who served in the Women's Auxiliary Territorial Service were popularly called 'ATS' or 'WATS'. The poem seems to recall a war-time Henley

'cheerioh' and 'cheeri-bye': the words have a war-time flavour. Greetings and leave-takings were frequent and moving, and these words catch the feel of the age

---

'Parliament Hill Fields' *New Bats in Old Belfries*

The poem opens with a description of the scene near Gospel Oak station, where the trains thunder under the road that runs up from Kentish Town to Highgate Village. Trams rumble over the bridge. There is a tram stop just outside Charrington, Sells, Dale & Co, the coal merchants. This was where the Betjemans waited at the end of a shopping trip into town. From the poor area of Kentish Town, the tram climbs upwards, through surroundings firmly imprinted on the poet's memory, to the terminus in smart suburbia. In the peace of the middle-class surroundings, Betjeman looks with pity on the poorer children who have gathered dandelions in the suburbs to take back to their rather squalid homes in Kentish Town. Their excursion has been in the reverse direction to his, from slum to leafy suburb.

NOTES AND GLOSSARY:
Betjeman was born in Parliament Hill Mansions and his parents moved shortly afterwards to a grander house not far away in West Hill, Highgate. Parliament Hill Fields is a stretch of public heathland where children play. Thus the tram journey up to West Hill in itself reproduces the social ascent of Betjeman's own family. He tells in *Summoned by Bells* how the atmosphere of nearby poverty was escaped when 'safe once more, we gained the leafy slope/And buttered toast and 31 West Hill'. He also tells how, as a child, he looked out from the window of the West Hill villa, hearing a train in the distance, and feeling 'Glad that I did not live in Gospel Oak'.

The basic metrical pattern here is an eight-stress trochaic line. Its effect, along with the emphatic rhyme scheme, *aabbb*, is to give to the poem the rolling, mechanical swing of a tram-ride. The heavy rhymes hint at the harsh grating noise made by the wheels on the lines.

Midland:	the old Midland Railway, later taken into the London, Midland and Scottish Railway, and then into British Rail
Nuts and nuggets:	Charrington's exhibited samples of coal in miniature railway trucks
Anglo-Norman:	the architecture of the building had something of the Norman style, with sturdy round pillars and semi-circular arches
bobble-hanging:	the plane tree has broad leaves and globular catkins
ashlar-speckled:	ashlar-stone is masonry cut in thin slabs used as facing

light suburban evening: the sunset blazes on windows and spire, making the bright scene a strong contrast to the sulphurous smoke of the train and the 'blackened girders' of the bridge, left behind on the tram-ride

Eighteen-sixty Early English: the Early English style replaced the Norman style when the round arch gave way to the pointed arch in the twelfth century. Early English became a favourite style for imitation by Victorian ecclesiastical architects

---

'A Subaltern's Love Song' *New Bats in Old Belfries*

This has become the most famous of the love poems addressed to sturdy athletic heroines. Here is another vigorous tennis-player from one of the fashionable southern counties. The strenuous singles which the poet has played against her have been a love-contest which he was delighted to lose. With her speed and her gracefulness she has defeated him almost casually; yet as a victor she loves him still. They chat as they walk back to the house to relax with a cool drink on the verandah and listen to the six-o'clock news. After that the subaltern has a bath and changes his clothes in readiness to take her to a dance at the Golf Club. She too has cast off her tennis gear, and he waits for her at the bottom of the stairs. Miss Dunn drives him to Camberley for the dance. They linger in the car park. The young lover has no wish to move. There they remain for the rest of the evening, and now the couple are engaged. This is a love story with a happy ending.

NOTES AND GLOSSARY:
Soon after the Second World War began, Sir Kenneth Clark (1903–83) found Betjeman a post in the Ministry of Information. One day Clark pointed out to Betjeman an attractive young lady who worked as a supervisor in the canteen. This was Joan Hunter Dunn. Here the poet assumes the role of a subaltern, a junior officer, aspiring to the hand of a senior

officer's daughter. Betjeman was himself in a comparably modest position when he aspired to the hand of Penelope Chetwode.

Aldershot: the home of the British army

euonymus: the spindle-tree, a shrub

six-o'clock news: this is war-time and the news bulletins were closely followed

Hillman: a popular make of small car

Egypt: presumably Joan's father had seen service in the army there; Egypt had been a British protectorate until 1922, and a British garrison remained there in the 1930s

Camberley: the site of the Royal Staff College; Sandhurst, the Royal Military Academy, is near by

ominous dancing: threatening an end to their privacy

'A Lincolnshire Tale'   *New Bats in Old Belfries*

The narrator is an Archdeacon, that is, a parson with a special responsibility for the discipline and well-being of the parish clergy over a large area of a diocese. His duty is to make official 'Visitations' to parishes to check up on the state of things both in respect of the condition of church property and of the conduct of services and parish affairs.

This Archdeacon is in the habit of taking a weekly drive into Wiss, the local market town. He is returning home. Sunset gives place to darkness on a spring evening with a chill in the air and a mist rolling down from the wold. In a narrow lane his pony suddenly drops dead. In this rather frighteningly remote area, surrounded by an intense stillness, the Archdeacon suddenly hears the tolling of Speckleby church bell. It is not a place he has ever visited because its rector is reputed to be mad. This fact adds a further touch of horror to the atmosphere. Speckleby is the site of a large country house now ruined, the village is being reclaimed by marsh, church and rectory are in a state of decay.

All is cold, dark, and sinister, as the Archdeacon stands among the tombs in the churchyard and sees the light of a taper through the leaded windows of the church. The sight gives him courage to open the church door. He is greeted by the smell of damp and dry rot. The church interior is a forest of brown woodwork, pews, and stalls reflected in the window panes; the plaster on the walls is dirty and flaky; the high old-fashioned pews are lined with baize; a massive three-decker pulpit rises menacingly over the nave. There is a sudden unforgettable silence as the bell ceases to toll. The door from the tower opens and the Archdeacon catches sight of the mad rector who has been the bell-ringer. The experience is so horrifying that the Archdeacon will never forget it – nor the wild rush away from the terrifying scene.

NOTES AND GLOSSARY:
There is a River Bain in Lincolnshire, but otherwise Betjeman has invented the place names. They exude a flavour of earthiness and angularity
appropriate to the area. The county is mostly flat, thinly populated in its
rural regions, much of the land made fertile by drainage.

The ballad-like form, with its anapaestic metre, conveys an air of
tension and excitement apt for the tale. The poem as a whole constitutes a
sequence of vivid exercises in verbal artistry. The tone of the first three
stanzas reproduces the comfortable self-satisfaction of the Archdeacon as
he drives home in the sunset. The phrase a 'whacking great sunset'
conveys his complacent mood of down-to-earth satisfaction. Then
suddenly the pony drops dead and the whole mood is transformed.
Betjeman builds up an awesome and eerie atmosphere. The vast intensity
of stillness amid the immense stretches of invisible fenland is broken by
the ominous tolling of the bell. All around the Archdeacon is the evidence
of decay and desolation, ruin and emptiness. And inside the church the
imagery of damp and rot suggests that the building and its contents, like
the estate, are being reclaimed by nature; for the pews are cavernous, the
roof is indistinguishable from the night sky, and the great pulpit frowns
like a massive grave-stone. The sinister, spooky atmosphere is alive with
menace and mystery.

tenor bell: in a peal of bells, which may amount to as many as
twelve bells, the largest is called the tenor bell

beasts in their fight: 'the lion and the unicorn fighting for the crown' on
the royal coat of arms

three-decker pulpit: fashionable in the eighteenth century; it could
accommodate the parson on the top level, the parish
clerk below, and a reading desk at the bottom

bands: a pair of white strips hanging down from the collar
worn as part of ecclesiastical, legal, or academic dress

'An Archaeological Picnic' *New Bats in Old Belfries*

The starting-point of the story is revealed in the last stanza. The poet and
Mary have just enjoyed a picnic in a meadow. Now the poet wants to
inspect the inside of the country church near by. The church is cool and the
weather hot. The poet urges Mary to leave the meadow, take her hat, and
finish her lemonade under the shade of the church wall or else in the
porch, where the church door-key is kept under the mat. He himself goes
inside the church, savours the smell of its tombs and floor-stones, lamps
and furnishings; and he delights in the stained-glass window designed by
Burne-Jones, through which the light gleams along the arches of the nave.
Meanwhile he leaves Mary to her very different pleasure of drinking
another bottle of lemonade.

NOTES AND GLOSSARY:

Betjeman's architectural enthusiasms made him an inveterate inspector of parish churches and other public buildings wherever he went. Mary's tastes do not extend to architecture; she is keen on the rather vulgar fizzy drink, but the words 'freckled innocence' in the last stanza suggest that she is a young girl and that the poet has no intention of ridiculing her. Rather, he seems to admire her patience.

Blunden time: the poet Edmund Blunden (1896–1974) wrote pastoral poetry which affectionately registers the detail of country life

Lady's Finger, Smokewort, Lovers' Loss: wild flowers

lin-lan-lone: see Tennyson's 'Far-Far-Away' – 'The mellow lin-lan-lone of evening bells'

rude forefathers of the hamlet: phrase taken from Thomas Gray's (1716–71) 'Elegy Written in a Country Churchyard'

cerements: strictly 'grave-clothes' but here used of the musty smell from ancient tombstones

Burne-Jones: Sir Edward Burne-Jones (1833–98), one of the Pre-Raphaelite artists; specimens of his designs for stained-glass windows are scattered throughout English churches

Trans arcade: the arches of the nave form a kind of arcade. Styles of architecture which come midway between one distinctive style and its successor are called 'transitional'. The word is used especially of the period when the Norman style was giving place to Early English

squinch: a stone giving support across an angle on a window or doorway

squint: a narrow aperture in a wall

'The Planster's Vision' *New Bats in Old Belfries*

This satirical study would appear to date from the war years. The speaker is one of those planners who is determined to modernise the country. He has no time for the traditional English village and its way of life. He surveys a typical rural scene which others might consider idyllic – trees, a church, and a huddled group of old cottages. He wants rid of it. The noisy church bells have called people to worship through the centuries, and too many people have been born and died here. The planner would replace habitations of this kind by scores of high-rise flats, their numerous windows glistening like silver. The pattern of individual cottage life will be replaced by mass-eating in communal canteens, where broadcast messages will proclaim the wonders of the new order.

NOTES AND GLOSSARY:
Betjeman clearly foresaw with remarkable accuracy some of the developments that were to be made in the 1960s in the way of housing and town-planning, developments which have now come to be regretted and condemned. By calling the speaker a 'planster' (where the dictionary word is 'planner'), Betjeman somehow makes the man seem even more repulsive, perhaps because comparable terms such as 'trickster' and 'mobster' are derogative. The last line of the first stanza, 'Carried the old their garden paths along', is illustrative of Betjeman's verbal subtlety. The grammatical inversions ('Carried the old' instead of 'The old carried' and 'their garden paths along' instead of 'along their garden paths') give the line the flavour of rather shabby old-fashioned verse which is too sentimental to be taken seriously. As such, it adds force to the planner's denigration of the past. The reader can detect the snarl of scorn and mockery in his voice. Similarly the patronising arrogance of the man comes through in his use of the word 'chum', which devalues the status of the person he is addressing. He reveals himself to be of the confident, no-nonsense, back-slapping breed.

the Challenge: this prophetic picture of brain-washed masses reminds us of how Big Brother keeps his grip on people in Orwell's *Nineteen Eighty-Four*, which was published in 1949

'Indoor Games near Newbury'   *Selected Poems*

The poet recalls a children's party he attended in a country house near Newbury. The poem is written in a jaunty, rollicking metre that reproduces the naïve excitement of the child. He fell in love with a golden-haired little girl, Wendy, and here he recreates the sheer ecstasy of dancing with her and then arranging to get together with her again after tea. They hid together in a cupboard in a bedroom, holding hands. This relationship is remembered as a love so pure and strong that he found it frightening. After the drive home the little boy hurries over his undressing and bathing, for it is only enclosed in the bed-clothes and drifting into dreamland that he can sense Wendy's continuing presence. And only then does the reader cease to share the child's feelings and to see him momentarily with adult eyes.

NOTES AND GLOSSARY:
Betjeman was a very genuine and touching recorder of childhood love between the sexes.

Bussock Bottom ...: the names are invented to suggest the rural Berkshire environment

Lagonda: a smart make of sports car

Rich the makes of motor whirring: this line introduces a passage which mimics the metre of Tennyson's 'The Lady of Shalott'

Victrola: a make of pianola, a piano which could be played in the normal way, or could have a perforated roll inserted that would work the keys mechanically

---

'St Saviour's, Aberdeen Park, Highbury, London, N'   *Selected Poems*

The poet is riding in a trolley-bus. He sees the network of sometimes criss-crossing wires threaded from standard to standard, diminishing to the eye in the distance, while traffic and posts and trees fly past the trolley-bus windows. Above all he sees the spire of St Saviour's church enlarging itself as the bus approaches it. This is where he leaves the bus, and it is a dreary, derelict area of London, with its forsaken, dilapidated shops, devoid of trade. Over this wasteland the Victorian church still stands, tall and bright in the evening sunshine.

This is the area which his parents knew in its more prosperous days, and he pictures what it was then like with its solid, Italianate, middle-class houses, their lawns and flower-beds, their stables, their separate entrances for tradesmen, and their broughams. Now these buildings are divided into flats and only the church remains what it was in the days when his parents went there, father in spats, mother in her flounced skirts, the days when the gentlemen doffed their top hats in greeting. Parents and grandparents also in their day trod these tiled floors and sat in their familiar pew in this very building to which the poet himself has returned. In this setting, which represents an island of continuity in faith and practice amid a sea of change and decay, the poet is moved by the significance of the consecrated bread of the Eucharist in which God himself is here and now sacramentally present; the very God who made the millions of people alive today, the poet included.

NOTES AND GLOSSARY:
This poem is written in hexameters, that is six-foot lines. Metrically the line is patterned on the classical hexameter, a form never widely assimilated by English poets because it does not always sit comfortably with heavily accentuated English scansion. Skilfully used, however, its slight strangeness and unexpectedness clothes what is said with a special dignity.

polychromatic: many-coloured

brougham: a one-horse closed carriage with two or four wheels for two or four passengers

tradesman's entrance: where tradesmen could make regular deliveries and be received by a servant. The front door was for the owner's guests

spats:	short gaiters covering the ankles and the tops of the shoes from rain
encaustics:	decorated tiles
stencilled:	decorated with designs and possibly also with inscriptions

Veiled in golden curtains: the Host, or bread consecrated at the Mass, is reserved in a small curtained tabernacle so that it can be taken by the priest to the sick

chain-smoking millions: an image for the masses of people imprisoned in the strange machinery of modern civilisation

---

'Beside the Seaside' *Selected Poems*

The title echoes the song, 'I do like to be beside the seaside'. In the inter-war years this was the signature tune of Reginald Dixon (1905–85), a popular performer on the Wurlitzer organ, whose recitals were regularly broadcast from the Tower Ballroom at Blackpool. The poem constitutes a lively social documentary on the typical annual summer holiday of a week or a fortnight at a seaside resort, which most English holiday-makers took in the 1920s and 1930s.

The poet looks first at the departure of families from their suburban and city homes. Class divisions are evident in their different modes of travel: by train, by a car made for the popular market, or by an expensive car. The sea lures them all; the whole nation seemingly moves out to the coast. Even as father's foot presses the accelerator, his toes itch to feel the sand between them. But the journey is not romanticised. Betjeman recalls that family travel involves children being sick en route and wanting to go to the lavatory.

The picture of the resort, Sandy Cove, is a generalised one – chapel, garden walls, promenade, shops, cafés, and the big hotel. There is a perceptive account of the family's lodging house, with its lack of provision for children on wet days and the fussy little regulations about tidiness and promptness.

Betjeman interrupts this amusing commentary with a lengthy and touching account of one little girl's private agony amid the jollity. We are taken into her heart and see a seemingly insignificant experience turned into the beginning of a 'life-long tragedy'. Mr Pedder, a schoolmaster, annually organises games for children on the beach. Little Jennifer cannot forget that last year she was his favourite. She charmed Mr Pedder, and her liveliness and attractiveness made her queen of the group. She is expecting immediate recognition by Mr Pedder and a joyful re-run of her triumph. Gradually it dawns upon her that she has lost her prime place in his affections. She and her brother and sister are gladly welcomed into the game but without any hint of special predilection for her. She has been displaced by a new favourite, Christabel, and she blames the glasses her mother has made her wear.

While the young thus delight or agonise in the exciting physical environment of the beach, the older ones sit with their books, play golf, or lounge in deck-chairs listening to the brass band. The overriding general preoccupation of the adults is with class. For our mode of transport, our accents, our clothes, and even our words of greeting or farewell all mark us. The bank manager and his wife note the behaviour of the Brown family and decide that Sandy Cove is going socially downhill. Yet in fact, the poet observes, the seemingly vulgar Browns probably have more money coming into the household than the snobbish Grosvenor-Smiths. And it is on the well-earned contentment of the Browns that the poet finally dwells, adding a note on the changelessness of the sea over the passing ages.

NOTES AND GLOSSARY:

Betjeman's achievement here is to recreate the atmosphere of a seaside resort in the 1920s and 1930s. It is done by a deftly selective accumulation of images covering the physical environment, the social nuances, and the feelings of holiday-makers, young and old. The strange blend of the comic and the pathetic is characteristic of Betjeman. The family holiday of the time might be something to make fun of in a superior way, but it was a crucial social experience in the lives of simple, hard-working parents and their young families. Like so many other human experiences on which Betjeman casts his observant eye, it tickles him, and yet he loves it.

Green Shutters . . . Windyridge . . . High Dormers: typical names given to suburban houses

Morris eight: a popular small car

Rovers: rather up-market cars at this time

macrocarpa: an evergreen tree used for hedges and windbreaks

Esplanade: the promenade running along the sea-front

escallonia: a flowering shrub

nowhere for the children: at boarding houses providing bed and breakfast it would be assumed that guests would be out all day, and the lack of provisions indoors discouraged return

Board of Trade: Jennifer joins the Civil Service, in those days a career for single women

B.T.M.: a squeamish euphemism for 'bottom'

Humoresque: a popular piece by Antonin Dvořák (1841–1904), it has often been arranged for café orchestras and brass bands

Rudge: the Rudge-Whitworth firm made bicycles and motorcycles

Flannel Dance: at which informal dress, such as flannel trousers, could be worn

'North Coast Recollections' *Selected Poems*

The poet stands on the coast in Padstow Bay, already described in 'Trebetherick'. The golf links are now deserted, for the sun is setting. Bray Hill is silhouetted against the sunset and its shadow (its 'phantom') stretches towards the church. The immediate surroundings are devoid of people. The locals are preparing for a dance. As the poet drinks in the scent, beauty and peace of the scene, he recalls that this is the coast where St Petroc landed and where Parson Hawker lived. At low tide here a stretch of sand is bared which was once part of the mainland and could be so again. Against this background of scenery pictured in the light of its long history, Betjeman gives us a series of contemporary snapshots alive with human detail.

Mrs Hanks's bungalow is to be the scene of tonight's dance. Her daughter Phoebe is trying to make the concrete floor smooth for dancing by rubbing it with French chalk. Norman and Gordon slide over it in their dancing shoes. The house appears to be a holiday home in view of Mrs Hanks's remark that for meals their habit is to pick up what they can find and picnic on it. As the youngsters make their preparations, the poet admires their health and vitality at this teenage stage of energy and puppyfat.

A second snapshot shows a little boy making for home, his bare feet trudging through the sand and his parents following him from their walk with the dog.

A third snapshot takes us to the local tennis court where Harold and Bonzo Trouncer are playing in the semi-finals of a tournament against a couple from the village of Rock. Bonzo's youthful beauty inclines Captain Myatt, the referee, in her favour. The Trouncers beat the visitors.

A fourth snapshot introduces young John Lambourn waiting for his beloved, agog with all the rapture of first love. When Bonzo arrives he cannot speak at first for the sheer depth and tenderness of his feelings for her.

The fifth snapshot takes us to the well-to-do home of the Wilders. Mrs Wilder is just finishing her reading of a bed-time story about the Arthurian knight Sir Gawain to her youngest child. The two young daughters, Primula and Prue, are still playing 'He' in the garden, hoping to postpone bed-time, while the eldest of the family, Harvey, is making a model boat in the garage. Mummy calls the girls in with a loud 'Coo-ee', and the two of them scamper off into hiding. Harvey is destined for the dance at the Hanks's.

After these pictures of life at Trebetherick, the poem ends with a coda. We see 'Jim' (perhaps the poet himself) on a September evening, after a storm, watching the water streaming down towards the sea, while the bell-ringers of Padstow send their chimes pealing across the estuary on their practice night. The sea reaches its final tide-mark on shore before it begins to ebb away.

NOTES AND GLOSSARY:
The concentrated little miniatures of daily social interchange and the short bursts of dialogue create a vivid sense of living human beings with individual warmth about them. Mrs Hanks's 'We picnic here' and Mrs Wilder's 'Mumsie wants you. Sleepie-byes!' have the authentic personal ring. And nothing could be more charged with suppressed feeling than the seemingly casual words which are all that John Lambourn can bring himself to say before his adored one: 'You going to the Hanks's hop to-night?'

lady's slipper: a flower, also called 'bird's-foot trefoil'

fairway: the smooth part of a golf course between the tee and the putting green of each hole

Bray Hill: or Brea Hill, rises on the coast just off Trebetherick

Stepper-wards: Stepper Point is the tip of the promontory on the further (western) side of the bay

Petroc: St Petroc, reputedly a Welsh king's son who went to Ireland to study, then crossed to Cornwall in a coracle, landed at Padstow, and founded a monastery. Several churches in Devon and Cornwall are dedicated to him

Parson Hawker: Rev Robert Stephen Hawker (1803–75), Vicar of Morwenstow, a village north of Bude and south of Hartland Point: poet and antiquary noted for his lively ballads which include 'And shall Trelawney die?'

'My sweet Hortense': the song on the gramophone record

Benares: a town in India which produces notable brassware

'Eiffel Tower': a brand name of soft drink

asbestos: the house is an asbestos building on a concrete base, a holiday chalet rather than a permanent home

Now drains the colour . . .: the line metrically echoes lines in Tennyson's lyric, 'Now sleeps the crimson petal'

pater and mater: Latin for 'father and mother'; terms once used in upper-class families with a public school background

Budleigh Salterton: an attractive Devon watering place with plenty of scope for outdoor games

Demon Sex: the feminine charms of Bonzo

Morris ten: a popular model of car at the time

rocks and stones and trees: see Wordsworth's poem on Lucy's death, where she is 'Rolled round in earth's diurnal course/With rocks and stones and trees'

Walter Crane: Walter Crane (1845–1915) wrote and illustrated many children's books

What time without . . .: Betjeman sustains the 'ye olde' idiom and word order of the tale Mrs Wilder has been reading. The archaic preciousness suits her; she finds the story 'So old, so lovely, and so very true!'

gypsophila: a genus of annual or perennial herb

Morris pattern: wall-papers designed by William Morris (1834–96) became very popular in the early decades of the century as part of the 'art nouveau' fashion

Wendy Hut: a miniature 'house' in the garden for children to play inside (Wendy Darling goes off with Peter Pan in J. M. Barrie's (1860–1937) play). The Wilders' household seems to be an affluent one

Ingersoll: wrist watch, made by the Swiss firm Ingersoll which dominated the English watch market at this time

---

'Harrow-on-the-Hill' *A Few Late Chrysanthemums*

On an autumn evening in London the poet is mentally transported from where he is in Wembley to his beloved Cornish coast. The tapping and the whispering of the poplars in the breeze is like the sound the little breakers make when the tide comes up in Padstow Bay. Harrow-on-the-Hill is transformed before his eyes into a rocky island, its churchyard holding buried sailors. The clicking and hissing of the trolley-buses makes it sound as though the level stretch between Harrow-on-the-Hill and Wealdstone is covered with surging waves, and the rumble of the nearby trains is like the plunging of rollers into the seashore caves. There is a storm-cloud over Kenton that seems to threaten a gale, and the lights of Perivale look like harbour lights. Glancing at the roof-tops along the skyline, the poet fancies them a fleet of trawlers rounding Pentire Point in Cornwall, hurrying to beat the coming storm into port at Padstow.

NOTES AND GLOSSARY:
Harrow-on-the-Hill is a couple of miles north-west of Wembley, and Wealdstone is roughly three miles north of Wembley. Kenton lies about two miles north of Wembley and Perivale lies just south-west of Wembley. From where he is standing the poet's eye sweeps round in an arc from Kenton to Perivale on either side of Harrow-on-the-Hill.

The emphatic rhythmic pattern, with its frequent use of feminine line-endings (strong followed by weak syllables, as in 'Wembley' and 'trembly'), would create a sing-song effect inappropriate to the subject, were it not for two facts. Firstly, Betjeman slows down the movement as each stanza subsides into shorter lines. Secondly, the emphatic rhyme scheme of the first stanza is subsequently tempered by more unrhymed lines: *ababxxxb*, *abxbxxxb*, *abxbxxxb*. The rhyme embodies an appropriate mood of excitement without sacrifice of dignity.

The archetypal modern lyric of nostalgia for the country in the middle of a busy city is 'The Lake Isle of Innisfree' by W. B. Yeats (1865–1939). In Yeats's poem the sound of lake water lapping by the shore is heard 'in the deep heart's core' and removes him mentally from the grey pavements of the London street. In Betjeman's poem the London scene does not stand in that kind of contrast to the longed-for rural scene. The London scene is itself transfigured before his eyes.

'Christmas'   *A Few Late Chrysanthemums*

The winter scene is set with images of stove, lamp-light, and rain. Betjeman then describes typical preparations for Christmas in a country village, a provincial town, and the centre of London. Meanwhile young men and girls of every class are sending off their Christmas presents and greetings. The preparations provoke the poet to ask, Is the Christmas story true? Was the Creator of all things born in a stable at Bethlehem? Because if it is true, it far outweighs in significance anything else in human experience.

NOTES AND GLOSSARY:
Betjeman took his religion seriously and would naturally have been conscious of the contrast between Christmas as the celebration of Christ's birth and the accretions that have gathered around it in the modern world. Not that they are disparaged; for they are pictured quite affectionately.

Advent: in the Church's year the period before Christmas, a
                       time of 'waiting'
Tortoise: brand name of an iron coke stove
Crimson Lake ... Hooker's Green: the names of colours
Dorchester Hotel: an expensive hotel for the wealthy in London
Bread and Wine: consecrated in the Holy Communion as Christ's body
                       and blood

'The Licorice Fields at Pontefract'   *A Few Late Chrysanthemums*

One of W. B. Yeats's best-known poems, 'Down by the salley gardens', begins 'Down by the salley gardens my love and I did meet'. It is a simple love song with a romantic turn of phrase. The loved girl has 'little snow-white feet' and a 'snow-white hand', suggestive of her delicacy and gentleness. Betjeman's transposition of the setting to the liquorice fields of Pontefract is a characteristic stroke of humour. And correspondingly he replaces the romantically pictured girl of Yeats's love-song by the sturdy-legged young woman in flannel slacks who has flaming red hair and sulky, sensuous lips. On the edge of a dingy industrial area, against a background of liquorice bushes, mills, and corner-shops, this red-haired hoyden makes the poet her slave. She grasps the weak, wilting, winded creature in her sturdy arms.

NOTES AND GLOSSARY:
Betjeman often has fitful echoes of other poets, but in this case he takes a particular poem and then comically turns its content and mood topsy-turvy. Pontefract, in the industrial West Riding of Yorkshire, was the most unromantic of sites to choose. For long its buildings were black with smoke from mill chimneys. Neither Pontefract cakes nor Liquorice Allsorts are confections with romantic associations. Liquorice blackens the mouth. Moreover it is used in numerous medicaments. These points are made because Betjeman was himself sensitive to social and psychological nuances in the gradings which are supposed to distinguish what is refined from what is vulgar.

Pontefract: the name itself is harsh on the ear
golden skin: this suggests that she has freckles
blazing eyes: the element of burlesque in the idiom escalates in the last stanza

---

'Essex'   *A Few Late Chrysanthemums*

The poet is studying an Edwardian book of colour-plates of Essex, and he is tickled by its precious, old-fashioned style. Words such as 'vagrant', 'erstwhile', and 'wend' carry the flavour of sentimental guide-books. Nevertheless its message touches him, informing him how once it was possible to walk from Benfleet to Leigh-on-Sea by rural footpath. Turning the pages of the book, the poet catches in his own words the quiet, idyllic scenes which were to be found in Essex before London's recent vast expansion got under way. Ponds, streams, by-roads, cobbled paths to cottage doors, together reflect the placidity of a past age. And the names of villages such as Havering-atte-Bower enhance the old-world charm. The book covers both the distant coastal areas of 'Far Essex' and the area nearer London where the River Lea flows south past Hertford right down to London, to join the Thames at Blackwall. Epping Forest lies to the east of the River Lea. It brings back special memories to Betjeman. On their periodic outings, his father's work-force sometimes went to Wormley by the River Lea on the edge of Epping Forest and Betjeman joined the employees in one of their coaches, while his father went by car. Breaks for drinks at country pubs were an important part of the jollifications. The last thought is of the local branch railway lines, their tracks now choked with weeds and brambles.

NOTES AND GLOSSARY:
Betjeman tells in *Summoned by Bells* how he early became an enthusiastic collector of old books, and the kind he most delighted in were books of plates with views of places as they were in the past. Here the pictures stimulate him to some highly perceptive descriptive writing through which, stanza by stanza, we get glimpses of vividly etched scenes, sharp in detail and very varied in character. Each stanza, after the first, catches a distinctive aspect of the county's scenery. The sheer economy of the descriptive style is remarkable. A few verbal brush-strokes, and the view is there, clear and alive.

erstwhile: formerly (*archaic*)
Benfleet: a few miles to the east of Leigh-on-Sea
Leigh-on-Sea: the name itself has an ironic ring, since the village of Leigh lost its identity long ago, having been swallowed up by neighbouring Southend-on-Sea
'A Summer Idyll Matching Tye': the poet is reading the titles of illustrations, as in other lines where there are double quotation marks
sucking mud: the marshlands of East Essex
convoluted: suggests that the pub buildings have been awkwardly expanded around an original small inn to meet rising trade
brakes: early motor coaches, or charabancs
half-land: the no-man's-land between the edge of London and Epping Forest
Great Eastern: The old Great Eastern Railway, with its terminus at Liverpool Street, covered the counties of Norfolk, Suffolk, and Essex

---

'Middlesex'   *A Few Late Chrysanthemums*

Elaine is a young lady returning home from London to the suburbs by the Central Line which runs through Ruislip Gardens. For the poet she is a symbol of the age that has replaced the age when this part of Middlesex was still a rural area. Her clothes, her hair, and her cosmetics mark her as a fairly well-to-do commuter. Her sandwich supper before the television screen fixes her in the late 1940s or early 1950s. Brooding on her way of life, the poet reflects on the Middlesex he knew before it was utterly suburbanised.

The River Brent flows through Ruislip and the poet recalls what it used to be like, with the meadows, trees, and footpaths along its banks. Northolt, Perivale, and Greenford were all taken into the borough of Ealing in 1901. Betjeman looks back to a time when each had its own identity, with hayfields, market-gardens, and the taverns where the anglers and sporting shooters used to refresh themselves. Among such, last century, were the Poshes and the Pooters now long dead and buried.

NOTES AND GLOSSARY:
Betjeman develops a favourite theme in contrasting what he sees as the suburban vulgarities of the age he lives in with the atmosphere of a quieter, less populous period. The 'red electric train' and the 'concrete station', not to mention Elaine's habit of saying 'Ta', all have a touch of crudity in the eyes of the sensitive aesthete. Elaine's clothes, toiletries, and cosmetics smack of modern mass-production and marketing methods offensive to old-fashioned refined taste. Betjeman's recall of the lost rural scene, however, relies to a certain extent on ready-made poeticisms like 'meadowlands' and 'mayfields' which carry a heavy freight of emotive nostalgia. The reference to the Poshes and the Pooters is noteworthy. Betjeman seems to have had a peculiar fondness for a celebrated series called *The Diary of a Nobody* which was originally published in *Punch* and then in book form in 1892. Written by George and Weedon Grossmith, it was supposed to be the diary of a simple-minded, aspiring gentleman working in an office in the business world. This is Charles Pooter with Carrie his wife and Lupin their son. Murray Posh is a rather showy fellow who comes their way. Betjeman celebrated the secure lives of the Pooters in his poem 'Thoughts on *The Diary of a Nobody*'.

lost Elysium:	lost Paradise
Windsmoor:	a stylish brand of women's clothing
Jacqmar:	a fashionable brand of silk wear for women
Drene:	a much-advertised shampoo
bobby-soxer:	contemporary equivalent of 'teenager'
Innoxa:	a brand of face-cream
Perivale:	an ancient village with a thirteenth-century church
Greenford:	an area of open fields until the early part of this century
bona fide:	Latin, literally 'with good faith', so here 'genuine'. Before 1914 the law was that *bona fide* travellers, but not locals, could get drinks at inns out of hours

---

'The Metropolitan Railway'   *A Few Late Chrysanthemums*

The poet is sitting in the buffet at Baker Street Station on the Metropolitan Line. He stares at the elaborately decorative electric lighting. The brightness of the vacuum bulbs symbolises for him the 'radiant hope' of the men who worked in the early days of electrification. The quality of the woodwork, the stained-glass, and the photographs on the wall corroborate his sense of the hope and idealism that marked the start of the electric railways system.

The poet tells the story of a couple which provides another human instance of 'radiant hope' now passed away. Long ago they used to ride from Ruislip, through the stations, Harrow, Preston Road, and Neasden, on their daily journey into the city. The young man worked in London Wall, a street in the commercial centre of London, the 'City'. He was cheered throughout his working hours by thoughts of his home. At lunch-time he would go to Farringdon (another station on the Metropolitan Line) and buy plants for his garden. Meanwhile his wife would be shopping in Oxford Street, also served electrically by lights and lifts. Perhaps it was here, at Baker Street Station, that they met for their return journey back to suburban Middlesex.

The two made a comfortable home in suburbia, determined to do their best for their children. But the husband died of cancer, and his widow is dying of a heart complaint. Their villa has gone, replaced by an Odeon cinema with its flashing neon lights. Baker Street somehow commemorates for the poet the love and hope of their early days.

NOTES AND GLOSSARY:

The Metropolitan District Electric Traction Company was registered in 1901 to electrify the Metropolitan District Railway. A year later it was absorbed into The Underground Electric Railway Company of London Ltd. There was a rapid development of the system in the next ten years. The electrolier, which becomes for the poet a symbol of the bright hope of those days, is a lavishly constructed cluster of electric lights. It is an elaborate piece of workmanship made of iron ropes decorated with copper hearts. As was customary with early electric lighting devices of that kind, the flex carrying the power is twisted around the metal chain and was not fitted into the framework while it was under construction.

The poem seems to tap a philosophical vein with its melancholy theme that early radiant hope gives way to grief. The account of the couple's personal tragedy has pathos. A parallel negative progress is implied in the development from the carefully designed electrolier that no doubt illuminated the couple's early meetings, to the crude neon lights of the cinema that has replaced their home. Fascinating as the poet's train of thought is, the basic parallel here is somewhat artificial. The human feelings of the reader that attach to the couple's sad story cannot be appropriately transferred to an account of developments in the electricity and transport industries. Betjeman himself nourished a peculiar set of enthusiasms. It is characteristic of him to try to fuse in a single poem the concerns of the railway buff and the poet's eternal lament on the passing away of human happiness.

electrolier: a word invented to match 'chandelier'

Bromsgrove Guild: a group of craftsmen whose handiwork included the gates of Buckingham Palace

Youth and Progress: these personifications, in the style of eighteenth- and nineteenth-century poetry, represent a now discredited poetic device; Betjeman's decision to juxtapose old-fashioned poeticisms with a story of travel on the Underground is characteristic

---

'Devonshire Street W.1'   *A Few Late Chrysanthemums*

Devonshire Street, like Harley Street, lies close by some of the major London hospitals. It is a smart street with dignified architecture. Perhaps nowhere is Betjeman's poetic technique more powerfully employed than in this poem. The presentation of events is imaginatively devised so as to make the maximum emotional impact. We first hear a heavy door closing, and the words that describe the sound, 'rich, sympathetic, discreet', convey something of the quiet, gentlemanly, undemonstrativeness with which consultants treat their patients. The outer scene is sunny and grand. But the couple leaving the consultant's house have just learned that the husband has terminal cancer, confirmed by the X-ray photographs he is carrying. There is 'no hope'. The words are repeated against a background of an external world wholly unmoved and indifferent – the calm, lofty house and its chimneys steady against the sky.

The husband puts his hand on the 'iron nob' of the railings, and envies it its chill insensitivity. The pedestrians hurrying by seem 'merciless' in their detachment from his tragedy, as he foresees a protracted and painful death. His wife puts her fingers comfortingly in his, exactly as she used to do long ago when they were young. The sheer humdrum ordinariness of what she says crowns the poem with an agony of irony. It is cheaper to take the tube to Piccadilly and then catch a nineteen or a twenty-two bus. The emotive power of this mundane touch of common sense is like that of King Lear's 'Pray you, undo this button', when he has found himself utterly bereft (Act V, Scene 3). It is deepened by the hint that money is also going to be a problem now.

NOTES AND GLOSSARY:
There is a technical adroitness in the placing of the word 'Shuts' at the beginning of the second line. This emphatic word marks a closure with total finality. It is not just a door that is being closed, but the life of one and the happiness of two. There is no trace of Betjemanian jog-trot in this poem. Simple sentence structure is deftly managed within the metrical pattern to preserve both dignity and naturalness. Even the clear, steady rhymes are unobtrusive. Indeed the poetic technique throughout this masterly registration of human crisis and grief is, like the sound of the closing door, 'rich, sympathetic, discreet'. In several poems Betjeman wrote directly about death, yet he never elsewhere touched the nerve of

human dread more harrowingly than here, where there is no waste of rhetoric on its horrors, but just a straightforward dramatisation of a human experience only too familiar to many people.

faience adornments: glazed earthenware and porcelain adornments
nob: an archaic alternative spelling of 'knob'

'The Cottage Hospital' *A Few Late Chrysanthemums*

The first stanza presents the poet lying in a walled garden on a hot Sunday afternoon. It is an idyllic scene, the trees heavy with fruit, the air alive with insects, and children at play in the street nearby. All is tranquillity and fruitfulness. In the second stanza a different aspect of nature's life emerges. A vivid account of a spider devouring a housefly is recorded with microscopic focus on the sheer ruthless savagery of the slaughter. And the poet observes wryly that no other being in the garden noticed the doomed struggle of the dying victim.

This thought introduces the powerful final stanza. The poet wonders where and how he himself will meet his end. Will it be in some hygienic cottage hospital, where nurses draw screens around the bed to shield his death from others? Will his groans and writhings recapitulate the struggle of the housefly, while natural and human life continues as usual all around the hospital?

Skilful transitions of thought make each stanza here a separate and distinct revelation: the first, of natural and human life at its most fruitful and pleasant; the second, of nature's brutality which that fruitfulness and pleasure tend to conceal and obscure; the third, of our inability to escape nature's inexorable cycle which for the individual ends in death. Betjeman does not moralise further. There is no generalised mention of 'Nature, red in tooth and claw', to use Tennyson's phrase, or of man's inevitable mortality. Instead, the respective scenes are vividly pictured and the reader is left to draw out the implications.

'Remorse' *A Few Late Chrysanthemums*

Betjeman gives us a touchingly straightforward account of his mother's death. He describes her last moments without any attempt to blur the grim anatomical realities. The death means the end of worry and waiting. It also means the withdrawal of someone whom the poet has loved and has left. The discreet professional bearing of the nurse, who is not unaccustomed to such events, puts the death into its context for the rest of the world as just one more in the daily count of mortality. For Betjeman, the event seems to disturb a whole series of accepted valuations. Religious differences once regarded as weighty seem trivial in the face of death. Yet his own past acts of neglect and unkindness to his mother now seem so burdensome that he

would gladly put up with more suffering at the bedside of death, if by
doing so he could ease his conscience.

NOTES AND GLOSSARY:

Distantly tender: she has that mixture of gentleness and detachment by
which the professional nurse protects herself from
emotional strain

'The Olympic Girl'	*A Few Late Chrysanthemums*

This poetic adoration of an athletic Amazonian woman comes from later
in Betjeman's life than previous similar outbursts. The poet admires a
large girl who can look down upon him from above. He longs to be worth
her attention, longs more ardently to be held close to her breast as she
holds her tennis racquet. The idea of being her racquet involves a wish to
be swung around in her arms. Banged against a ball, he would be taut-
stringed in her hands, and eager to feel his strings snapped by the vigour of
her play. The match over, he would flop on the ground at her side and she
would tuck him up inside the press. The dream fades as the poet recollects
that he is too old to be able to attract her.

NOTES AND GLOSSARY:
The comic way in which Betjeman develops the image of being a tennis
racquet in the hands of the loved one is a mixture of self-parody and sheer
farce.

retroussé: the polite term for a tilted 'snub' nose
freckled: this seems to be a common feature of the girls Betjeman admires
would I were: translation of the Greek; the line exactly repeats a
line in Rupert Brooke's (1887–1915) 'Grantchester' –
'. . . would I were/In Grantchester, in Grantchester'

'The Dear Old Village'	*A Few Late Chrysanthemums*

The title is ironical. Betjeman vents his satiric ire on aspects of modern
life, more especially in their effects on the traditional English village,
which is supposed to be a picture-postcard centre of beauty and
tranquillity. The church bells ring out unmusically, for only three of the
peal of six are in operation: there has been a row about the ringers' tea,
and three of them have gone on strike as a result. This introductory symbol
of disharmony and dissension sets the tone for the portrait of the village
that follows. It is evening (for the sunlight is being scooped into the
western window panes) and it is Sunday. The bells are calling to worship;
but they call in vain, for 'we are free to-day', says the poet ironically,

mocking contemporary attitudes; we have thrown off the shackles of religion and feel no need at all to praise the Creator of our beautiful world. The old Victorian hymn tunes cannot compare with up-to-date pop music. Nature and God are both outmoded concepts since the dawn of atomic science.

The poet turns his attention to the realities of the contemporary village. Farmers have wired off the public footpaths, which makes it difficult to get to church anyway. In the street young men tune up their motor-bikes and girls with painted lips and nails hang about, waiting to sit astride a pillion. These youngsters will not be going to church, but to the local road-house with its mock-Tudor bar, and to the cinema which now opens on Sundays. Only two old ladies and a four-year-old child can be seen making for the church.

Since this is the age of progress, let us forget about the surrounding hills and streams and the new birth of spring in the earth around us, and let us focus on the progressive people who have replaced their ancestors. With this pronouncement the poet turns his attention to one of those who has made the village what it now is. He points to a smart late-Georgian farmhouse. Its thatched outbuildings have gone, replaced by a Dutch barn and concrete cowsheds. Its owner, Farmer Whistle, is a wealthy man with a well-stuffed paunch, and he is an adulterous braggart, a liar, and a thief. His wife brought money with her, but he neglects her for a mistress he keeps in the nearest town. He sits on the Rural District Council where he agitated for better rural housing. Then, under the pretence of being helpful, he sold what is really a useless, undrainable piece of land to the Council for three times what it cost him. Now hideous council houses occupy this unworkable land: they are jerry-built, the wind blows through ill-fitting doors, and rain-water floods the floors. The knowing locals privately call the estate 'Whistle's Win', but if anybody seriously tries to take on the farmer and expose his dishonesty, then he gets his revenge through the War Agricultural Committee. Farmer Whistle's real contribution to local life consists in throwing rubbish in a neighbouring pond, closing off footpaths, letting walls drop to pieces, and neglecting rented cottages until they fall into ruin. It is useless to try to take legal action against him because he is on the local bench of magistrates.

The poet points to the village school, a building put up in 1860 but now, in 1947, no longer in use. In the supposedly bad old feudal days the villagers were ruled by three people: the squire, the parson, and the schoolmaster. It was the schoolmaster who knew the villagers most intimately. The poet is thankful that he is no longer alive to witness what has happened. Progress has shut the village school and all the children are taken by bus into a town eleven miles away. It is with a scornful pen that Betjeman describes the educational diet now provided for the young in hygienic glass-walled buildings: civics, eurhythmics, economics, and the rest. Being turned into 'Citizens of To-day', they will learn to scorn the village environment that bred them. Girls aspire to jobs in Woolworth's instead of in households and boys to driving tractors. This is the age when all are prescribed an eight-hour day, of which at least three are spent in tea-drinking, in idle chatter, and in listening to radio music. The squire, the parson, and the schoolmaster may turn in their graves; but it is thus that we have freed ourselves from their tyranny.

Turning from today's youth in the village to today's adults, the poet takes a moral line in his judgments. There is Mrs Speak who has lived for fifteen years in the same house with her husband's widowed sister without speaking a word to her. The three of them dwell in a quaint old cottage which to look at would be a water-colourist's dream. There is Mrs Coker and her large brood of children, four of them fathered by her husband, two by Farmer Whistle, and two by coloured American servicemen now back in the USA. Mrs Free, an outwardly prim personage, is the village gossip and the source of this unsavoury information.

As for the men, their husbands, there is no time to explain which of them are honest or dishonest and which of them thrash their wives. You must go to the local inn on a Friday night to listen to them. There they sit, getting drunk at the expense of a field-worker who is making enquiries about village life. The drunker they get, the more they fabricate tall stories for their visitor. But these villagers are clever enough to take in a sophisticated sociologist, making him think he is really in touch with the rural scene and the rural mind.

NOTES AND GLOSSARY:

Lin-lan-lone: taken from Tennyson's 'Far-Far-Away – 'What sound is dearest in his native dells?/The mellow lin-lan-lone of evening bells.'

fane: an old word meaning 'temple'

DYKES: John Bacchus Dykes (1823–76), a prolific writer of hymn tunes, many of them still popular

BING: Bing Crosby (1904–77), American crooner of the day

atomic energy: in 1947 the scientific world was agog with the wonderful possibilities opened up by the prospect of nuclear power

Lift not your eyes: Betjeman is ironically adapting the opening of Psalm 19: 'I will lift up mine eyes unto the hills'

doxy: mistress

War Ag. Committee: the War Agricultural Committee had power to control what local farmers were allowed to produce and to get provisions for

behold the Village School: Betjeman seems to have in mind Oliver Goldsmith's (1730–74) poem 'The Deserted Village'

which gives a sentimental account of the Irish village
he knew as a child before depopulation and recalls
the parson and the schoolmaster especially

"Music while you work": a popular war-time radio programme designed
to boost the morale of workers

coloured fathers in the U.S.A.: large contingents of US troops were in
England prior to the invasion of Europe

Hillman Minx: a popular model of small car

'Wantage Bells' *Poems written after 1954*

The poet listens in Wantage to church bells ringing on a Sunday morning
in spring, conscious of the nuns at prayer in their chapel. His attention is
focused on the abundance of flowers around him: the walls covered with
roses which seem to act like sounding-boards and send the tones of the
bells rebounding across the fields; the heavily-scented wallflowers and the
numerous other flowers and weeds that are taking over from the primroses
and hyacinths. The sheer reckless profusion of new life represents a divine
generosity for which no words of thanks could be adequate. Even the song
of the birds cannot express the degree of gratitude which we owe for what
is so unstintingly given. Only the notes of the bells sound a kind of praise
whose flowing clarity matches that of the brook.

NOTES AND GLOSSARY:
As a response to the rich display of beauty in nature, this poem recalls the
work of Gerard Manley Hopkins (1844–89). The recreation of the beauty
around the poet has the vividness and vitality which are found in Hopkins,
but there is a significant distinction between the two poets. Hopkins's
response to the beauty around him would be a paean of praise to God.
Betjeman's religious response is implicit rather than explicit. The words
'bestowing' and 'thanks' imply a giver and a duty of gratitude, but God is
not mentioned. We are intended to take the point that, while the nuns are
worshipping within, the world of flower and stream and bird outside is
ablaze with beauty which calls for response.

The stanza here is ingeniously devised. It has a rather heavily flowing
rhythmic pulse in keeping with the sound of bells. The judicious mix
of shorter and longer lines (four-foot with two-foot in the first stanza,
three-foot with two-foot in the two other stanzas) culminates in a final
longer five-foot line. The rhythmic pattern created suggests a sequence of
'changes' from a peal of bells.

Sunday-ly: this 'portmanteau word' combines 'suddenly' with
'Sunday'

nuns: the Anglican Community of St Mary the Virgin at
St Mary's Convent, Wantage

'Hertfordshire'   *Poems written after 1954*

This poem recalls a humiliation that long rankled in Betjeman's mind. His father was given to outdoor sports and often went with a companion on shooting expeditions. On this occasion they went to Buntingford in Hertfordshire, taking John with them. Shooting expeditions were hateful to young Betjeman, who scarcely knew how to hold a gun. He disgraced himself by clumsily firing into the ground. As a result his father was deeply pained, and John had to endure his recriminations as they were driven back home by car.

The poet has this sad memory in mind as he revisits Hertfordshire much later in life. There are still some remnants here and there of its former rural beauty: the cornfields, the elms, the thatched cottages, the water-mills, and the flint churches. But generally the landscape has been transformed for the worse by the encroachment of London; there are wires above, new towns on the ground, estates of brick, and concrete lamp-standards. Betjeman reflects wryly that this disfigurement would have pained his father even more than his own clumsiness with the gun.

NOTES AND GLOSSARY:

knickerbockered: wearing knickerbockers, the sporting trousers gathered in just below the knee

syndicated shoots: gentlemen would join together to rent the right to shoot for a season over a certain area where game was to be found

Lionel Edwards: an artist (1878–1966) who painted hunting scenes often in dull, cold weather

Rover Landaulette: a motor vehicle in which the passengers could be exposed to the air behind the driver (as in the old Victorian horse-drawn landau)

'Lines written to Martyn Skinner'   *High and Low*

The poet calls Skinner to return to Ealing. Betjeman was of course a city-dweller as well as a lover of the countryside. Skinner had decided to leave Oxfordshire because it was too noisy. Betjeman calls him back to London. The ironical appeal of the poem lies in Betjeman's cunning way of turning the accepted town–country relationship topsy-turvy. To forsake the country is to leave tractors, nuclear reactors, and roaring motor-cyclists behind, to escape the din of lorries grinding up rural lanes in low gear and jet planes practising low flying overhead. It is to exchange these raucous distractions for the leafy avenues where birdsong can be heard, for the tranquil Sunday morning sound of church bells and the milkman's greeting.

NOTES AND GLOSSARY:

Martyn Skinner (*b.* 1906) was one of Betjeman's contemporaries at Oxford. They went up to the same college, Magdalen, on the same day. Both became poets and both turned their backs on literary modernism, cultivating a direct poetic style and traditional metrical forms. Skinner wrote a satirical epic poem, *Merlin, or the Return of Arthur*.

Betjeman's use of the familiar expression, 'smoothly glides', generally used of a rural stream, for the movement of an urban bicycle illustrates his gift for revitalising what might seem to be a spent verbal currency.

Return, return: the rhythm of the first four lines is that of the popular hymn 'Stand up, stand up for Jesus'

'Harvest Hymn'   *High and Low*

This poem parodies the popular harvest hymn 'We plough the fields and scatter/The good seed on the land', which celebrates the annual cycle of sowing and reaping as the source of all that is healthy and nourishing. Betjeman mimics the metre and phrasing of the hymn, and turns it into an ironic glorification of the modern farming methods and attitudes that he hates. The use of poisonous sprays, the destruction of wild flowers, the battery system for hens, electric fences, concrete sheds, and the farmer's dependence upon his television and his deep-freeze – all these features of the modern rural scene are condemned. Alongside the attack on modern farming methods goes an attack on the mercenariness of modern farmers. Their farming methods are chosen for their profitability. They treat land as their private property rather than as an inheritance to be protected. If they cannot make money by growing crops, then they will sell their land for building sites.

'Meditation on the A30'   *High and Low*

The poet takes us into the mind of the kind of road-hog who uses the car with its vast speed and manoeuvrability to vent his personal frustrations, anger, and contempt for others. He has quarrelled with his wife; he presses down on the accelerator, the saliva in his mouth bubbles as he puffs at an unlit pipe. Resentment with his wife makes him determined to assert himself against the lorry and the Mini that prevent him from speeding away. Fury with his wife's attitude is transformed into fury at the resistance to his will represented by the traffic ahead. He begins to desire an attractive young woman to replace his wife, and at that movement a driver behind him blows his horn. The irate motorist thinks it unworthy to be overtaken by anything less grand than a Jaguar. His anger rises, his determination to be in front escalates to a climax, and he roars round the vehicle ahead to his death.

NOTES AND GLOSSARY:
Betjeman was a traditionalist in his poetic techniques and in his attitudes to modern life. Yet he did not limit himself as a poet to the more obvious subjects conventionally accepted as the proper material for poetic treatment. Here he brings his traditional technique to bear upon a situation all too familiar today, death in a road accident caused by sheer human conceit and silliness. The ingredients make ripe material for a poet – anger, arrogance, emotional turmoil, and consequent tragedy.

dottle: a plug of tobacco left unsmoked in a pipe

'Inexpensive Progress'   *High and Low*

Betjeman's indignation is at its fiercest in this poem. It shows him out-raged by developments which the majority of his contemporaries regarded as 'progress'. His assault is directed at features of the modern environment which many conservationists now deplore. He condemns the damage done to the countryside by electricity pylons, by the destruction of hedges, and by the building of motorways, with their hideous signs. The sacrifice of beauty to the cause of speedy travel irks him, and he mocks the feeble attempts to mitigate the damage by arranging patches of lawn in service stations and rockeries on roundabouts.

The development of air travel has been as damaging as the development of road travel. Villages are sacrificed in order to construct runways, while cheap war-time huts, half-ruined, are left to litter the countryside. In the town there is comparable defacement of old streets by the chain stores, with their crude facades, and by the traffic that thunders through them. It is a waste of time to try to preserve a bit of greenery here and there in a country where power stations can be located anywhere. The final stanza sees the environment of the modern road, with its hideous lamp-standards and its lurid vapours emitted from the monstrous vehicles we travel in as a kind of hell. To be in it is to be as good as dead.

NOTES AND GLOSSARY:
The short lines, the rolling rhythm, the emphatic rhymes, and the brisk declamatory style together produce a sense of seething anger.

floribunda: a kind of rose

'Executive'   *A Nip in the Air*

This poem is a dramatic monologue. That is to say, a fictional character speaks throughout, and in speaking reveals what kind of a person he is. The form is peculiarly suited for satirical use. It works particularly well here because the character in question is exactly the kind of person who likes to talk about himself and his doings. He is full of self-confidence. He is making a success of life, as he supposes and by his own standards. But everything which he says positively about himself can be taken negatively by the reader. It is precisely the things he boasts about which the poet despises and ridicules.

In entering into the mind of the pushy, self-assertive business executive, Betjeman mimics the vocabulary and idiom, even somehow the tone of voice, of the up-and-coming managerial type. It is done with great skill. This is one of Betjeman's later poems, and he is portraying the kind of business representative who emerged in the late 1960s and early 1970s. The humour of the piece, of course, lies partly in the touch of exaggeration and distortion. For instance, 'basically I'm viable' sounds all the funnier because, though the kind of person in question would over-use the words 'basically' and 'viable', he would not in fact put them together to describe his own daily activity. In the same way, although the kind of person satirised would drive without proper consideration for others, he would not announce that he marked 'Pedestrians and dogs and cats ... down for slaughter'. Betjeman's sense of humour, in instances of this kind, gets the better of his eye for satirical accuracy.

NOTES AND GLOSSARY:

Cortina: the Ford Cortina was a model much used for company cars in the 1960s

maîtres d'hôtel: head waiters; the executive is proud of his bit of French

No soda, please: at this point we first learn that the executive is in a hotel bar, chatting to a fellow-drinker

mild developing: Betjeman turns the executive in his spare time into the kind of man he hates most. He dabbles in property, works on local planning officers, and if any old property stands in the way of his plans and the preservationists seek to keep it there, he colludes with the Borough Engineer and slaps a 'dangerous structure' notice on it. It is by this kind of dubious dealing on the side that he makes enough money to buy a speed-boat

Part 3

Commentary

Betjeman as a topographical poet

Betjeman seems to have been fascinated by places. He regarded himself as a topographical poet, and he expressed his admiration for predecessors such as George Crabbe (1754–1832) and William Barnes (1801–86). But what strikes us when we compare Betjeman's work with theirs is that, like most topographical poets, they focused firmly on their chosen locality, Crabbe on Suffolk and Barnes on Dorsetshire. Yet, although there are several poems by Betjeman which describe the area of Cornwall in which the family had their holidays, a general survey of his topographical poetry would take the reader to any number of places scattered about the country from Croydon and Exeter to Pershore and Harrogate.

Although a given locality seems in many cases to inspire Betjeman with its own particular spirit, he does not always register features of its landscape with great precision. In 'Dorset', for instance, Betjeman makes no attempt to picture the Dorset countryside. There is 'grass between the beeches' and there is a 'yew-tree bough' in the churchyard, but that is the limit of natural description. Dorset country life is represented by a handful of images that might apply anywhere – 'Horny hands' that hold the plough and gentler hands that milk the cow. The 'feel' of Dorset is created by nothing more than a list of resonant place-names and a calling-up of the spirit of Thomas Hardy in verbal and rhythmic echo. Nevertheless the reader could not possibly fail to carry away a sense of something that gives Dorset its special character.

By contrast 'Essex' gives us a series of snapshots that bring features of the scenery vividly before the reader. The visual realisation of the county's character is conveyed through a number of colour-plates, each given verbal equivalence with delightful economy and clarity. 'Upper Lambourne' too registers the particular scene in sharp focus. The poet follows where the light of the sun leads with a watchful eye, and when the focus settles on the gravestone of the celebrated trainer, Betjeman gives a human interest to the scene not present in 'Essex'. It is not a particular human interest; no personal story emerges. It is rather a generalised human interest pertaining to the widespread, swelling downlands. They survive from pre-history while generations of horses and trainers move away 'out of sight and mind'. There is a philosophical dimension here, where in 'Essex' the reflective content was simply regret over the changing environment.

Wordsworth tells us how his early interest in nature was renewed and revivified when he began to look at the hills and rocks and streams, and to hear at the same time 'the still sad music of humanity'. There are few unpeopled landscapes in Betjeman. And it is not just the world of nature that he peoples so as to remind us of life's vicissitudes. The urban scene is treated in the same way. One of the most popular of Betjeman's early poems is 'Death in Leamington'. In this poem, again there is a minimum of descriptive effort to bring the Spa externally before the eyes; just a reference to peeling stucco and Italianate arches. What happens inside the bedroom is the stuff of the poem. Nurse comes in with the tea-tray; she bolts the window, unrolls the blind, lights the gas, and mends the fire. All this might happen anywhere. But Leamington Spa is useful to Betjeman as a background because it is associated with bygone upper-class life, with fading gentility, and with the steady progress of the elderly to the grave. Thus to die is made to seem a most natural way in which to spend an afternoon in Leamington Spa. Nurse takes it all calmly enough. Yet the voice of the poet presses home in a series of questions the ultimate fragility of peeling plaster and failing heart alike.

If the human spirit of Leamington Spa seems best represented by a quiet death in the afternoon, the human spirit of Henley-on-Thames is best represented by beefy ATS girls shooting through the bridge. In this case the scene is painted with a deftness of observation that crowds the reader's vision with colour and vitality. Moreover, the poet himself is present this time: it is his shared personal sensitivities that draw us into responsiveness to what is pictured. There is energy here that makes the perfect contrast with the stagnant languor of 'Death in Leamington'.

Deaths, however, are not infrequent in Betjeman's topographical poems. The early poem 'Croydon' distinguishes Croydon as the place where Uncle Dick was born and died. There are exact local references in the sense that the school Uncle Dick walked to has a name, the woods he played in have a name, and the street he lived in has a name. Such names in themselves, however, carry firm associations only for residents and people familiar with the place in question. For others they merely suggest a precision which cannot be properly tasted. This is not to suggest that nothing would be lost from the poem if 'Croydon' became 'Bradford' or 'Bolton' and the other names were adjusted accordingly, for Betjeman gives us glimpses of the 'Coulsdon woodlands,/Bramble-berried and steep' and tells us that the 'laurels are speckled in Marchmont Avenue'. It is these images that do the main work of poetry. The names feed in an ingredient of seeming exactitude to a total picture which coheres all the more memorably in the mind.

Both 'Death in Leamington' and 'Croydon' could fairly be defined as poems in which death gives significance to places, but there is a certain ambiguity about the death in 'Exeter'. While it may be argued that, with its air of decayed gentility, Leamington Spa is an appropriate place for an old lady to die in, it cannot be said that a cathedral city such as Exeter is an especially appropriate place for a car-mad doctor to smash himself up in. In this poem the spirit of the place is realised in a series of images that bring the cultured calm of the cathedral city before us. Yet the human story raises problems. The doctor's wife has intellectual pretensions, is reading the latest highbrow novel, and has become neglectful of religious practices. The doctor is a road-hog and pays the penalty for it. His wife is bereaved and takes up her religious practices again. There is surely too much material here for a poem of five stanzas. The doctor's fate is a story in itself, and Betjeman tells something like it impressively in 'Meditation on the A30'. As for his wife's story, we need to know either more or less about it. As it is presented, it makes the reader ask, What is the poet getting at? Does he want us to grieve or to laugh?

The proportionate relationship between the scene painted and the human interest explored varies enormously in Betjeman's poems of place. Sometimes the one swamps the other. Sometimes the two are well balanced. 'Love in a Valley' might be cited as a case where the fullness of scenic presentation all but swamps the human story. The situation explained in the last four lines can scarcely make its proper emotional impact upon the reader after the fervid onrush of emotive delight in the journey and the arrival. 'Take me, Lieutenant' is a call with a light-hearted flavour. The rhythmic imitation of Meredith suggests that the poet is having fun. The cascade of imaginative description that follows is riotously profuse. After being immersed in it, we are scarcely ready to adjust ourselves to the brief reference at the end to the Lieutenant's coming departure for China. We want to know more of this matter, which seems to belong to a poem with a soberer tone, a poem that would not have swung us along at such a rollicking pace.

'The Metropolitan Railway' might be cited as a poem where the description of place and the human story which arises from it are better balanced. The transition from the sketch of the buffet to the story of the doomed couple is neatly effected by the poet through his attention to the sepia views of Pinner on the buffet wall and his consequent reflections on the journey from there to town. The story is concisely but fully told. We are not left wishing at the end either for more information about the couple or for a fuller picture of the buffet. Topographical and human interest are proportionately balanced. But that does not mean that they are in all respects harmoniously blended. Few readers will be able fully to share the poet's feelings when he makes sadness about the fate of the once confident couple applicable to the career of the electric railway line. In order to be fully in sympathy with Betjeman the topographical poet, the reader is asked sometimes to assume feelings for railway trains and railway stations that are not easy to acquire.

Betjeman's nostalgia for childhood

Childhood memories became a source of poetic inspiration for Betjeman as they did for Wordsworth. Wordsworth's memories, of course, were concentrated in the Lake District. Betjeman's experience left him with acute nostalgia for the two very different environments of London and Trebetherick. In this respect Betjeman is certainly a poet of town and country alike. There have surely not been many poets who would give comparable romantic treatment to memories of the sea-coast and to memories of urban railway stations.

Perhaps the word 'romantic' needs to be qualified in speaking of Betjeman's memories of childhood. He did not conceal the miseries of being bullied at home and at school in *Summoned by Bells*. Nor did he falsely idealise recollections of holidays in Cornwall. The scenes conjured up in 'Trebetherick' are not only alive with realistic details of sand in sandwiches and wasps in tea, they also reproduce the awesome dread of childhood in the face of the remoteness, the darkness, and the loneliness that nature sometimes has to offer. The children's terror of the evil reaching out from Shilla Mill reminds us of young Wordsworth's flight by boat from underneath the towering peaks above Ullswater. There is an exciting ocean at Trebetherick which can wash up treasures at your feet; but its thunderous power in a storm can hurl the children against each other with the force of a blizzard. In more ways than one the children's experience of the sea portends what adult life may have to offer.

By contrast 'Parliament Hill Fields' records memories of urban delights. Instead of the 'yellow foam-flakes' blown up the cliff, we have sulphurous smoke rising into the sunset. Instead of thundering waves we have thundering trams and trains. These are enjoyable excitements for children. As the description in 'Trebetherick' reached a climax in the hurly-burly of the storm, so here the noisy, rocking tram-ride marks the culmination of the shopping expedition. After it there is comparative calm. Having swept past a panoramic array of buildings, we are safe in well-to-do suburbia. And here the thought takes a sharp turn. Where 'Trebetherick' ended with a rather sentimental recollection of old friends, 'Parliament Hill Fields' ends with a disturbance registered in the child's thoughts and feelings. He has made the journey from the squalid to the respectable, and he cannot but pity the children who are going in the opposite direction – from an afternoon in suburbia back to home in the slums.

Among Betjeman's poems of childhood are some which recollect the first childish taste of love for the opposite sex. This is a difficult experience for an adult to recapture in words without lapsing into what is mawkish or even absurd. Yet the revelatory jolt which first love can give to a young child is often unforgettable. In 'Indoor Games near Newbury' Betjeman manages to present such an experience at a children's party so sensitively that the intensity of the little boy's inner romantic upheaval is fully realised – 'Love so pure it *had* to end' – and yet when it is all over and the little boy is put to bed at night, Betjeman manages to restore the readers to their adult viewpoint and to indulge a smile as the child nods off to dreamland.

We see young love from the little girl's side in 'Beside the Seaside', though here we are confronted with a slightly older child than the little boy who hides in a cupboard with Wendy. We cannot pretend, however, that Betjeman is exactly recording his own experience when he takes us into little Jennifer's mind as she experiences the tremendous let-down of no longer being the chosen favourite she was a year ago. Nevertheless only a man deeply affected by his own memory of childhood suffering could explore a little girl's feelings so sympathetically. For the most part, however, 'Beside the Seaside' interests us for what is directly personal to the poet, his memories of the annual holidays. Indeed there are passages of the poem in which the child's view is paramount:

> We, in turn
> Pass poorer families hurrying on foot
> Towards the station.

We go to 'Our lodging-house'. But the child's angle is not sustained. Betjeman looks at the typical holiday resort with sly adult glances at the social pretensions of the various grades of visitors. And three-quarters of the way through the poem 'we' becomes 'We older ones'.

The major attempt to recapture in verse the experience of long-past holidays in Cornwall is made in 'North Coast Recollections'. While in the account of John Lambourn's meeting with Bonzo, Betjeman once again gives voice to the overwhelming experience of young love as he had known it, the rest of the poem presents a cross-section of life in the seaside resort for the young people staying there.

Frequently Betjeman's nostalgia for places he knew as a child is touched with grave criticism of the changes that have since transformed them. In 'Middlesex' he laments what modernity has done to the rural Middlesex of his youth. In doing so he extends the range of his criticism beyond the reach of memory. For the lives and characters of the Pooters, which are cited in contrast to the life and character of Elaine the commuter, do not belong to Betjeman's boyhood. *The Diary of a Nobody*, recording the doings of the Pooters, was published in book form in 1892 and had already appeared in *Punch*. This is how Betjeman's mind seems to have worked. He speaks of the 'gentle Brent' he knew in childhood, yet his regret for what has gone takes in a way of life that was thirty years in the past by the time he was ten years old. Similarly we notice in 'Essex' that what causes the poet to regret the changing face of the country is a collection of plates illustrating an 'Edwardian Essex' that really preceded his own early memories. In 'Hertfordshire', on the other hand, Betjeman's focus is on a real past that he himself knew, for the regretted country scenery is inescapably tied to painful early experiences touching his relationship with his father.

Recollection and narration

Poems of personal recollection represent only one category in which Betjeman excelled. In some of the poems of place, such as 'Trebetherick' and 'Upper Lambourne', the element of personal recollection is paramount. In others, however, such as 'Middlesex' and 'Exeter', personal recollection gives way to an objective interest in other people. The narrative element is strengthened as the element of personal recollection is reduced. Yet, in both poems of recollection and of narration, Betjeman was able to transfigure experience with heightened emotional and imaginative intensity.

'Harrow-on-the-Hill' is a poem of pure recollection. It is not a 'poem of place' in the sense that it makes any attempt to present Harrow realistically to the reader. Indeed Harrow is significant here only because it can be imagined to be somewhere else. Some critics have assumed that Betjeman is recording a childhood memory of how one evening the London scene was transformed into his beloved Cornish scene. Whether the experience belongs to childhood or not, Betjeman's treatment of it is very skilful. Acute aural sensitivity is revealed in the way the whispering of the poplars, the hissing of the trolley-buses, and the rumble of the train are transformed into the sounds of the sea on the shore. It is as though Betjeman has decided to take 'Trebetherick' and 'Parliament Hill Fields', and to blend the memories they call up into one. In a sense, the poet of the town and the poet of the country here resolves the dilemma of his dual enthusiasms. This is a poem packed with images that appeal to the senses and the heart, metre and stanza form are cunningly crafted, and there seems to be no word wasted.

By total contrast Betjeman tries his hand at pure narrative in 'A Lincolnshire Tale'. As we should expect, it is a narrative poem drenched in the flavour of a particular locality. What is more surprising is that it moves from a naturalistically pictured Lincolnshire into a world of Gothic horror, a world we associate with writers such as Thomas Hood (1799–1845) and Edgar Allan Poe (1809–49). Ruined mansion, tolling bell, tombs and taper, damp, rot, and the spectre-like madman – this is the stuff of the horror novel. It might seem no more natural to be suddenly transposed from a solid Lincolnshire roadway into this world of gruesome decay and sinister darkness, than it was to be transposed from gazing at Harrow-on-the-Hill to gazing at Padstow Bay. Yet just as the whispering trees and hissing trolley-buses in Wembley sparked off an exit from one world into another, so the autumn mist in Lincolnshire, the silence all around, the feeble glimmer of the carriage lamps, the death of the pony, and the sound of the church bells together whisk us from the everyday world into a world of terror. Harrow in the evening was transfigured by vision into the Cornish coastline. Lonely Lincolnshire at night is metamorphosed by dread into the scene of a nightmare.

Betjeman's versatility is remarkable. To turn from this narrative poem to another poem of personal recollection, 'An Archaeological Picnic', is to enter a totally different literary world. Surely it represents Betjeman personally at his most winning. It shows his architectural interests indulged to the full, and yet it puts this hobby into the context of a delightful human relationship to which it is irrelevant. Architecture is the poet's passion; to explore an old village church is happiness. Yet Mary, it seems, could not care less. The poet's taste for the technicalities of architectural criticism is of no interest to her at all. She would rather have another bottle of lemonade than talk about Burne-Jones. The poem fascinates us as much because of what it does *not* do as because of what it does do. Betjeman was a master of vituperation when it came to expressing his scorn of the world's artistic philistines. Yet here there is no breath of disapproval; just a simple, straightforward, humble acceptance of the girl's 'innocence'. This is a personal poem *par excellence*. It is totally lacking in pretension. It is the stuff of daily life. It makes us aware of the poet's genuineness. It makes us like him.

If the poet in person is there to make good company in 'An Archaeological Picnic', he is totally absent from 'The Arrest of Oscar Wilde at the Cadogan Hotel'. Here we have a remarkable degree of objectivity in dramatic presentation. It would be difficult in this poem to put one's finger on a line or two where the voice of the poet comes through, clear and unmistakable, in some sort of judgment upon the scene, whether sympathetic or moralistic. Rather he gives us a series of tableaux, each with its own dramatic tang. The picture of the drinking poet and the unmade bed is followed by the picture of Wilde frothing away in conversation about *The Yellow Book*, the quality of the hotel service, and his wardrobe. The reader is left feeling at once impatient with Wilde and apprehensive about what is to follow. But the entry of the policemen is pure burlesque. They are comic-strip cockney figures who talk as though they are hamming their roles. What does Betjeman want us to feel? Are we to guffaw at the farcical comedians? Even as we ask the questions, the farce gives way to tragedy. The final picture is a starkly unnerving study of a staggering, ruined man. The poet has mixed up the truly incongruous ingredients of the Wilde story into an extraordinary dish which he serves up without any comment at all.

Betjeman had a sure touch in dramatic presentation. We saw it in the delightful snapshots of Trebetherick life in 'North Coast Recollections'.

We see it in what is perhaps his gravest poem of all, 'Devonshire Street W.1'. Betjeman displays a poetic interest in death in 'Death in Leamington', in 'Croydon', and in 'Exeter'. But the deaths there are not events to touch the heart as the events of 'Devonshire Street W.1' do, though, strictly speaking, it is not a poem about death itself. It is about something more terrifying to most men and women – that moment in life when the prospect of a future is dashed to pieces by the news that one is terminally ill. Shakespeare once observed that a man who kills you does at least confer one great blessing on you: he deprives you of years of fearing death. So Betjeman's most sombre poem is not descriptive of death, but of how the news is received that death must come. What is especially moving is the presentation of how the blow falls on a man and a woman in the ordinary workaday world of a London street. There is little in the way of direct utterance of agony: just the very natural question, 'Why was I made for this?' and the awareness that hurrying people all around belong to a now remote and alien world. Otherwise emotion is conveyed wholly by symbol and implication – by the comforting fingers of the wife, by the cold stone of the palisade, above all by the closing of a heavy door.

Poems of indignation

Betjeman had strong predilections and they were balanced by corresponding disapprovals. His enthusiasm for Victorian architecture was matched by his hatred of cheap modern buildings; his enthusiasm for railways was matched by his hatred of motorways; his attachment to the quieter, friendlier suburbs and villages of his childhood made him critical of the depersonalised new towns and industrial estates. His memories of the business manners of an earlier generation made him impatient with the human representatives of modern commerce and technology. These various predilections and distastes appear in some of his poetry in a fairly unobtrusive way; but sometimes he lashes out at what he hates with bitter vituperation or jaunty ridicule, or indeed with both.

Sometimes Betjeman's satire is alive with good humour. As an Anglo-Catholic he wrote many poems in which he poked gentle – or not so gentle – fun at fellow Christians suspicious of his kind of churchmanship. He could be equally critical of irregular Anglicans who treated their Church less than seriously. The 'Diary of a Church Mouse' represents this genre in *Collected Poems*. Entertaining as much of this humorous satire is to those aware of what it is all about, this vein did not produce Betjeman's best work.

There are, however, poems where the voice of indignation is so powerful and the target of the satire so justly defined that they have been accepted as among Betjeman's most memorable efforts. 'Slough' is a case in point. The sheer clarity and directness of the declamation and the hectoring rhythmic forcefulness are irresistible. Added spice is given to the sweeping condemnation by the exaggeration of calling down aerial bombardment on the profiteers and their handiwork. There is the same gross exaggeration in 'The Planster's Vision'. The irony here is heavy. Instead of pouring direct ridicule and condemnation on the planner – as he did on the bosses at Slough – Betjeman makes him condemn himself out of his own mouth. It has to be accepted that the planner does not and never did exist who would call for wholesale destruction of villages, complaining that too many poeple have been born and died in them. But it is a fair technique employed by the satirist to say: 'Look, this is what your attitude amounts to. You may not be aware of it; but you are taking sides with the builders of a crude, depersonalised Orwellian Utopia.'

A more comprehensive assault on modern progressivism is contained in 'The Dear Old Village'. Again the irony is heavy, for the 'dear old village' is now a seething hotbed of selfishness and vice. There is no attempt here to contrast the wickedness and ugliness of the town with the innocence and beauty of the rural village. Indeed the complaint seems to be that nowadays all the corruptions of urban life have spread out and infected rural communities. In his poem 'Michael', and elsewhere, Wordsworth represented industrial cities as places of vice and depravity where an innocent young villager might be totally corrupted. But in Betjeman's poem, modern scepticism has invaded the village, replacing hymn-singing by pop music. Country girls have the nylons and cosmetics of townswomen and will go off to a road-house on pillions behind their boyfriends on a Sunday.

It must be said that Betjeman's satire is less clearly targeted in this poem than in some of his best. To regret that concrete cowsheds have replaced thatched barns is to lament a change in taste from one age to another. But to point out that a wealthy farmer keeps a mistress and has fathered illegitimate children is a very different matter, for no doubt this sort of vice has been a feature of village life in all ages. The necessary distinction between social and moral satire is here blurred. It is fair enough for the traditionalist to contrast the supposedly 'bad' (but in his view good) days of the feudal past, when the squire, the parson, and the schoolmaster ruled the village, with the destruction of the village community today. The replacement of the village school by the large comprehensive school a long bus-ride away is a social change which the satirist can fairly condemn if he wants. But this kind of social judgment of a historical character is not wholly compatible with moral judgment of a universal kind which condemns vice, theft, and corruption. It is one of Betjeman's weaknesses in some of his satirical verse that there is no proper discrimination between one kind of satirical target and another. He decides at the beginning of a poem to attack a given development, but, as he writes, other dislikes well up in his mind, so that, by the end of 'The Dear Old Village', for instance, mass-observation and sociology have taken their place alongside religious scepticism, cosmetics, adultery, administrative corruption, eurhythmics, and Marxism, not to mention tractors, motor-bikes, and branches of Woolworth's, all in the same bag of things to be mocked.

By contrast, the attack on modern farming methods in 'Harvest Hymn' is all the sharper for the restriction of focus. When Betjeman turns from his assault on the use of fertilisers and battery houses to picture the comparative affluence of farmers, the connection is justified by the fact that high-production techniques are adopted for their profitability. The irony of mocking the rhythm and phraseology of the well-known harvest hymn is ingenious. The farmer, like the planner in 'The Planster's Vision', is the spokesman. It is always a more subtly effective satirical technique for the target of ridicule to condemn himself out of his own mouth. If criticism and ridicule come directly from the mouth of the poet, then the poet is transformed for the reader into an angry, hectoring person. Betjeman avoids this risk in a variety of ways. In 'Slough' he avoids it by comic exaggeration: we *know* that the poet does not seriously want the place bombed. We are not, therefore, just listening to an angry man; we are listening to a man with a sense of humour too.

Sometimes Betjeman the satirist mixes the direct technique with the indirect technique. The first stanza of 'Meditation on the A30' is a piece of direct narrative by the poet. So are the last two lines of the final stanza. But in between we are listening to the voice of the driver. The bulk of the poem is a dramatic monologue – we are taken into the driver's mind, where we float on the stream of his consciousness. There the mental preoccupations of his domestic emotional situation thread their way through his reactions to the immediate matter of negotiating his way through the traffic. The poet does not directly pass judgment. He himself makes only two statements, introducing the angry driver and then telling us that he killed himself by overtaking at the wrong moment. The meat of the poem is sandwiched between these two statements of fact.

'Executive' is a pure dramatic monologue. There is no word from the poet in our ear here. We are in the presence of the executive and he reveals all we want to know about himself, and more. This is technically in direct contrast to poems such as 'Inexpensive Progress', where the poet vents his spleen on what he hates in straightforward vituperation without the intrusion of a distinctive persona or spokesman.

Poems of personal grief and faith

Throughout Betjeman's work the autobiographical element is strong, and yet there remains something elusive about the poet's innermost personality. We seek vainly in Betjeman for the degree of frank self-revelation that we find in Shakespeare's love sonnets, Wordsworth's nature poetry, and Donne's religious poems. There are, however, one or two poems which touch directly on a deeply personal matter which shadowed his later life, namely his early relationship with his parents and subsequent alienation from them. There was clearly a careless lack of consideration of his parents in Betjeman's wasteful way of life at Oxford, and the disappointment he gave to his father's ambitions for him eventually produced a sense of guilt. 'On a Portrait of a Deaf Man' takes us to his father's deathbed. Betjeman could not but recognise there that it was his father who, by taking him for country walks and arranging the holidays in Cornwall, had initiated him into some of the great passions of his life. Moreover, his father's deafness cried out for sympathy. The strange power of this poem lies in its total evasion of any overt expression of feeling at all, although in the last stanza the poet directs a seeming complaint at God. Otherwise the poem is a series of factual statements made in a style of unaffected simplicity. The deafness emphasised by the title becomes a symbol of the inadequate communication between father and son. But no sentiment is voiced, no open word of sorrow or guilt or regret. Instead every recollection of Betjeman's father as he knew him is in turn displaced by the sombre picture of his present condition as a corpse. Each contrast explodes in the reader's mind with reverberations touching the universal human future in the grave.

A different note is sounded in Betjeman's poem about his mother's death, 'Remorse'. The very title points to a feeling of guilt never explicit in the poem on his father's death. Betjeman's relationship with his mother seems to have been complex. He felt a deep love for her which he failed to give expression to, seemingly because he wanted to detach himself from what he saw as the superficialities and trivialities of her life. (He examined them in Chapter VIII of *Summoned by Bells*.) The direct admission here of his 'neglect and unkindness', however, somehow fails to carry the emotional weight of the unuttered feelings implicit in 'On a Portrait of a Deaf Man'.

Betjeman speculates about his own death in 'The Cottage Hospital', but the train of thought here is too 'clever' and contrived for the poem to be analysed for its emotional implications. If we want to see Betjeman at his most gravely serious in respect of human destiny, we have to follow him into church. There, in 'St Saviour's, Aberdeen Park, Highbury, London, N', his deepest religious convictions are voiced. What stirs them is the physical environment, and it is not a natural environment. The presence of the divine, which mystics and poets such as Wordsworth detected when they were overcome by the beauty of natural scenery, is felt by Betjeman in a place where generations have worshipped, and is located sacramentally in the consecrated bread of the Mass. There is no mention of God in 'Trebetherick' or in 'North Coast Recollections'. Betjeman's faith was inextricably involved with the institutional worship of the Church.

The death of his father made him wonder whether he could square this faith with the facts of human mortality. But Betjeman's was not a vague spirituality. It was a set of formulable beliefs clearly spelt out in terms of God's incarnation in Christ and in the continuing life of the Church. This is explicit again in the poem 'Christmas'. Not that the poem is free of all trace of lurking doubt. If the drift of the poem on his father's death was 'Can the Christian faith be true when life is so awful?', the drift of 'Christmas' is 'Can the Christian faith be true when its facts are so wonderful?'

Perhaps Betjeman's finest religious poem is 'Wantage Bells'. And perhaps it is the finest because it is not explicitly religious at all. God is not mentioned – any more than grief is mentioned in 'On a Portrait of a Deaf Man'. Betjeman is content to let the reader drink in the beauty of the scene, smell the flowers in their profusion, and then, taking a hint from the bells' invitation and the nuns' response, ask the question, How can gratitude for such generosity be properly voiced?

Betjeman's sense of humour

Betjeman has been regarded by some unsympathetic critics as primarily a writer of light verse, yet when we look back on the poems treated in this volume we find that there was most to praise in some of the most serious poems, such as 'Devonshire Street W.1', 'Harrow-on-the-Hill', 'Essex', 'Upper Lambourne', 'Trebetherick', and 'Wantage Bells'. It is a mistake to describe Betjeman as a 'comic' poet. There is much to make the reader smile in Betjeman's satirical sketches of people and practices he dislikes, as we have seen in 'The Planster's Vision', 'Executive', 'The Dear Old Village', and 'Slough'; but these are in no sense 'comic' poems. And amusing as it may be to see the words of 'We plough the fields and scatter' turned into an outburst in praise of poisoning the environment, the message of 'Harvest Hymn' too is deadly serious. Indeed the poem is an exercise in scathingly scornful denunciation.

There is one group of poems, however, in which the comic tone seems to predominate. They include a handful of Betjeman's most popular poems. What makes them distinctive is that they are, in a sense, 'love poems'. We say 'in a sense' because they are like no other poet's love poems. Betjeman sings the praise of a muscular, athletic woman. Such is Pam in 'Pot Pourri from a Surrey Garden'. She has a 'bountiful' body, she is 'mountainous', with strong 'hairy' arms and large thighs. What the poet 'adores' is her physical might and the 'arrogant' and 'petulant' gestures that mark her swipes with the tennis racquet.

This taste for the role of adorer from below of a half-disdainful Amazon is generalised in 'The Olympic Girl'. The 'sort of girl' the poet admires is a girl looking down on him from a great height with a hint of distaste,

indeed of fury at his presumption. Now the psychologists are ready to
pounce on such admissions as evidence of a 'masochistic' streak; but
Betjeman's development of the theme is so absurdly hilarious that such
theorising must inevitably be lost in laughter. For the poet yearns to be the
very racquet in her hands, swished and flung and banged around. The
image of being tucked up into a press finally reduces the subject to pure
farce.

Perhaps the most successful of the humorous love poems is 'A
Subaltern's Love Song'. Here the situation is developed into a little
narrative. The poet feels 'weak' from the loveliness of Joan Hunter Dunn
in her victory at tennis, but he is not wholly glad to have been defeated,
and far from escalating into farce, the poem develops into a charming
account of an evening tryst that culminates in engagement. Nevertheless,
the comic tone is maintained, partly by the repetition of the girl's name,
and its development from 'Miss J. Hunter Dunn' in the first stanza into
'Miss Joan Hunter Dunn' as events progress. The rollicking rhythm and
the firm rhymes play their part in creating an air of excitement.
Expressions such as the cry:

> Oh! full Surrey twilight! importunate band!
> Oh! strongly adorable tennis-girl's hand

are so much the stuff of self-conscious poeticising that the whole situation
retains a jokey flavour.

In 'The Licorice Fields at Pontefract' the comic tone is determined from
the start by the mockery of Yeats's 'Down by the salley gardens'.
Pontefract is not a romantic place and liquorice is not a romantic delicacy.
Yeats's poem speaks tenderly of a girl with little snow-white feet, and it is
impossible not to recall the fact when Betjeman admires 'the strongest legs
in Pontefract'. The Olympic girl was unattainable and Miss J. Hunter
Dunn had to be wooed, but the blazing-eyed heroine of Pontefract
seemingly takes the initiative, seizes the poet in her sturdy arms and
reduces him to a wilting weakling.

Perhaps the most distinctive brand of humour in Betjeman is the humour
which intrudes unexpectedly into a serious context. The mention of the
'Murray Poshes' and 'Lupin Pooters' at the end of 'Middlesex', intruding
on a passage of quiet nostalgia, is a case in point. They are rather absurd
characters from a rather absurd book. Moreover their lives were no less
representative of a shallow, regimented human consciousness than is the
life of Elaine, the contemporary commuter. To regret the passing of the
Pooters and their like in this context is absurd, and we know that the poet
knows that it is absurd. But his knowledge is not the same as his feelings:
they hanker after 'Pooterdom', silly as it may be. Thus Betjeman shares
his inner self with his readers in a way that disarms criticism. It helps to
make him a lovable poet.

A significant aspect of the mention of the Pooters is also its unexpectedness. Betjeman seems to enjoy giving the reader a sudden jolt by a quick change of tone. There is such a jolt given in 'Dorset' when the names of T. S. Eliot, H. G. Wells, Edith Sitwell, and other contemporary notabilities are listed among the dead in the Mellstock churchyard. Up to that point in the poem the reader has been comfortably settled in enjoying the picture of an idealised Hardyesque Dorset countryside. The shift of tone is disturbing to the reader. The question arises – 'Is this funny?' And what follows in the text, after this question has been raised, is taken with a pinch of salt. Moreover, the change of tone is retrospectively effective. It throws back on what has gone before a question mark about the degree of seriousness.

Betjeman uses this device in 'Love in a Valley'. The poem is as richly drenched in romantic feeling and romantic imagery as is Meredith's poem which it echoes. But two words unsettle the reader. The first word is 'Lieutenant' and it occurs in the first phrase of the poem. A girl does not address her beloved by his military rank. Would it be better, we wonder, if she had used his name? But 'Take me, Augustus' sounds silly, and 'Take me, my dear one' sounds too obvious. However, as we listen to the young lady and detect the spiritedness of her personality, we lose ourselves in her emotional fervour and forget her odd first words. But then, four lines from the end, she addresses the beloved again, this time as 'Portable Lieutenant'. Is this the idiom of an amorous young lady? Is she making fun of his commitment to do duty overseas? The questions are unanswerable. The mingling of the serious and the sincere with the seemingly facetious is an aspect of Betjeman's poetry that gives sauce to it. Sometimes it leaves readers feeling that they are being purposely teased and that the poet is relishing their discomfiture.

Occasionally, however, the question arises whether the intrusion of the comic or facetious element into a poem is really in good taste. With most poets we know exactly when they are being funny and when serious. There would probably never be an occasion, on reading Wordsworth or Tennyson, when we might ask, 'In what tone of voice should this line be read?' or 'Is it just possible that the poet is pulling our leg?' One of the student's difficulties in first encountering Betjeman's work is that occasionally these questions will arise. We have hinted that they arise in reading 'Exeter'. Certainly it is comic to hear how the 'doctor's intellectual wife' reads a book 'writ by A. Huxléy', and that kind of talk puts us in an amused mood. But then what are we to make of the 'smiling corpse' of her husband taking up the space formally reserved for the glossies? Are we still to be amused? It is, of course, possible to treat death comically. When Hilaire Belloc writes, 'Lord Finchley tried to mend the Electric Light/Himself. It struck him dead: And serve him right!' there is no ambiguity about the humour. Belloc does not confuse the mood by introducing us to the widowed Lady Finchley, and telling us how bereavement renewed her neglected religious practices.

There would appear to be some conflict in 'Exeter' between the mood established in the rather jaunty first stanza and the ultimate content of the poem. By observing the slight failure of cohesion here, we can more fully appreciate the perfect blend of form and content, style and tone, in poems as different as 'Henley-on-Thames', 'Parliament Hill Fields', 'A Lincolnshire Tale', and many others.

Versification

One quality which contributes a great deal to the success of Betjeman's best poems is his rare versatility at versification. He was well-read in Victorian poetry and cheerfully borrowed rhythmic patterns and stanza forms from poets such as Tennyson and Meredith, A. E. Housman and Henry Newbolt. But when he borrowed, he made the rhythmic patterns his own. And more important than his indebtedness to others was his gift for devising stanza forms to fit the substance and mood of his poetry.

There are poems where a deft craftsmanship blends content and rhythm with a peculiar felicity. 'Wantage Bells' has a stanza form and rhythmic pattern which send the changes of the bells pealing through the presentation of the scene, exactly as they would in reality. There is a vivid rocking tram-ride heard through the metrics and verbal music of 'Parliament Hill Fields'. And the roar and surge of the sea seem to beat the cliffs and eventually pour over into the lanes through the cunning arrangement of sound and image in 'Trebetherick'.

These, of course, are cases where special effects are called for by the presentation of actual sounds from bells, trams, and the sea. Less obvious perhaps is the relationship between form and substance in 'Henley-on-Thames', where all the colour and variety of the river scene are caught in a metrical movement which seems to ebb and flow like the rippling of the Thames between barge and bank. To appreciate Betjeman's versatility in this respect, it is only necessary to compare the hectoring rhythmic bombast of 'The Planster's Vision' with the quiet simplicity and economy of utterance in 'Upper Lambourne', or to compare the deliciously tranquil and conversational directness of 'An Archaeological Picnic' with the pulsing rhythmic rapture that transfigures the vision in 'Harrow-on-the-Hill'.

Part 4

Hints for study

Exploring the content of poetry

Every poet has his own special interests. When you study his work you will naturally want to define them. If you are studying a substantial work, such as a Shakespeare play or a Victorian novel, the matters to which you have to give your attention are confined within the single work. And within that work there will be a certain homogeneity. You will not have to ask yourself, as you turn from one scene of the play to another, or from one chapter of the novel to another: 'What kind of a work is this?' But when you are asked to study a selection of poems by a given poet, you cannot guarantee, as you turn from one poem to the next, that there will be any continuity of interest in respect either of subject matter or of authorial attitude.

With some poets this would not present much of a problem to the reader. They confine themselves to a narrow range of concerns when they put pen to paper. Betjeman, however, was a poet with a wide range of interests. He gave his attention as a poet to places of all kinds and people of all kinds, as well as, of course, to his own personal life. The number of topics which the student can explore in reading Betjeman is remarkable, as the list below indicates. We shall see too that the variety of needs and postures assumed is correspondingly rich – as indeed is the variety of poetic forms which accommodate them.

Whatever poem you may have to write about will have certain features linking it with other personal poems. You will write most interestingly about poetry if you learn to explore these linkages for yourself. It may be necessary to dig below the surface to discover connections that are worth exploring, because sometimes connections between poems are of a superficial nature and would not lend themselves to fruitful enquiry. For instance, 'Parliament Hill Fields', 'Middlesex', 'The Metropolitan Railway', and 'Devonshire Street W.1' all have a London location. But this would not be a fruitful connection to explore, for it is too vague and incidental to the central substance of the poems in question. It would be far more rewarding to link 'Parliament Hill Fields' with 'Trebetherick' or 'Indoor Games near Newbury' as poems involving memories of childhood; to link 'Middlesex' with 'Essex' or 'Hertfordshire' as poems about the changed English environment which Betjeman regrets; to link 'The Metropolitan Railway' with 'Exeter' as poems in which Betjeman conjures up a little human story while his mind dwells on a particular local scene; or to link 'Devonshire Street W.1' with 'On a Portrait of a Deaf Man' as poems about death.

The categorisations suggested above are certainly not either exhaustive or exclusive. While 'Hertfordshire' is linked with 'Middlesex' in being about the changed environment, it is linked also with 'Trebetherick' and 'Indoor Games near Newbury' in conjuring up childhood memories.

You might find it a useful exercise to pick a poem and show how it is linked to a variety of other poems by a variety of different points of connection. Consider 'Hertfordshire', for instance. It is linked with 'Essex' and 'Middlesex' (regret at the changed environment); with 'Parliament Hill Fields', 'Trebetherick' and 'Indoor Games near Newbury' (memories of childhood); and with 'On a Portrait of a Deaf Man' (Betjeman's relationship with his father). Similarly 'The Planster's Vision' is linked with 'Middlesex' and others by its regret at the changing environment; with 'Executive' in employing the technique of the dramatic monologue; and with 'The Dear Old Village' by its ironical content and its employment of satirical exaggeration. Again, 'North Coast Recollections' is linked with 'Upper Lambourne' by its vein of philosophical reflection on the sweep of history and on the way the natural environment outlasts human generations; with 'Trebetherick' by its concern with the identical environment; and with 'Indoor Games near Newbury' by its focus on early experience of love.

T. S. Eliot insisted that a poet's work must be judged as a whole. It is not necessary to study everything a poet wrote in order to get a comprehensive view of his interests and attitudes, but it is necessary to get into the habit of observing the kind of linkages we have discussed (and there are many others). A poem does not exist in isolation. A reader would get a very incomplete idea of Betjeman as a poet if he or she had not sampled a variety of poems on different themes. It is when we take a given theme and trace how it recurs in different poems that we are enabled to thread the poems together in our minds. As we do so, what at first looked like numerous isolated poems are seen as pieces woven together in a single fabric.

Below we cite a number of topics from which students can select suitable starting-points for detailed exploration of Betjeman's work.

Specimen topics for detailed study

1. The variety of the localities that appealed to Betjeman's imagination.
2. Betjeman's particular attachment to the scenes of his childhood, urban and rural.
3. Betjeman's way of linking particular places with individual human stories. How does this enrich the appeal of his poems on localities?
4. Betjeman's nostalgia for the Victorian and Edwardian ages.

5. Betjeman's insight into the child's mind.
6. The stimulus given to Betjeman's poetic imagination by the scenery of the Cornish coast.
7. Betjeman's fascination with London and the life lived there.
8. Betjeman's hatred of modern developments in building, transport, and the environment.
9. Betjeman's interest in conservation and what is now known as the 'green' movement.
10. Betjeman's awareness of suffering and death.
11. Where in Betjeman's poems does he reveal most of his inner self?
12. Betjeman's skill and effectiveness as a satirist.

Style, tone, and mood

To get the most out of poetry you should read it aloud. By the very nature of Betjeman's style, especially his use of firm rhythmic patterns and shapely stanzas, his poems lend themselves peculiarly well to being read aloud. The relationship between the mood of a poem and the swing or march of the metre makes oral delivery a special pleasure. But in order to read a poem intelligently – whether aloud or to yourself – you must fully appreciate what we have called the 'mood' of the poem. That means, in the first place, realising who is speaking and with what kind of attitude or feeling. The poet does not always speak in his own voice. The speaker in 'The Planster's Vision' is a planner vehemently expressing views which the poet detests. He is an unpleasant, dislikeable fellow, and in uttering his words, the arrogance of the man, his inhuman dismissiveness of the lives of villagers, will naturally be registered by the reader. By contrast, the speaker in 'A Lincolnshire Tale' is an Archdeacon, uncomplicated in his normal attitudes, but of a sensitive, nervous disposition. He has been benighted in a remote, eerie place. It was a terrifying experience, and the memory of it haunts him.

There are, of course, many poems in which the poet speaks directly to the reader. He does so in a quietly reflective mood in 'Essex', turning the pages of an illustrated book, and sharing his thoughts about it with the reader. He does so in an outraged mood in 'Slough', in a brooding mood in 'Upper Lambourne', in a jaunty mood in 'Dorset', and in a mood of excited reverie in 'Harrow-on-the-Hill'.

On the other hand, he seems almost to disappear out of reach of full understanding in 'Exeter', so that we are tempted to ask, 'What exactly is he saying to us?' This is quite different from what happens in 'Devonshire Street W.1' where the poet has become a totally anonymous narrator: his personality is obliterated, and we are left in the presence of two living characters, feeling what they feel at a time of almost unbearable tension and grief.

We have seen how fruitful understanding of what Betjeman has to say as a poet will be furthered by tracing thematic relationships between poem and poem. In the same way, sensitive appreciation of Betjeman's technical qualities will be developed by tracking from poem to poem common techniques of presentation, similarities in the use of vocabulary and imagery, and varieties of metrical experimentation.

Below is a list of topics by which aspects of Betjeman's style could be further explored.

Stylistic topics for detailed study
1. Betjeman's metrical versatility.
2. Betjeman's use of the dramatic monologue.
3. Betjeman's skill at matching form to the substance of his poems and the mood required.
4. The vividness of Betjeman's quick snapshots of people in action.
5. Betjeman's skill at brief descriptive sketches of scenery.
6. The significance of proper nouns in Betjeman's poetry – the names of places, people, streets, firms, and brand-names of goods.

Specimen questions and model answers

1. Show how Betjeman's early memories of Cornwall became a source of poetic inspiration.

Betjeman's early holidays in Cornwall left him with some of his happiest memories. In 'Trebetherick' he recaptures the delights that he and his young companions experienced when they played together on the coast. He recalls how they ate their picnics while watching the sea beat against the cliff below them. The recollections are vividly conveyed. We see the 'yellow foam-flakes' drifting like sponges on the ledge below and then lifted up by the wind over the cliff-top. We are also made to feel the discomforts of a picnic where sand gets into the sandwiches and wasps into the tea. It is not just the clarity of the poet's visual memory that brings the scene to life, but his recollection of how it felt to tread on the squelching bladder-wrack and have the sun beating on sodden bathing costumes.

There is a healthy lack of sentimentality in the reminiscences. The child's experience of the area was not all unmodulated joy. There was fear too. Our eyes are turned from the immediate scene to the woods way off where the children have seen pheasants and rabbits killed by foxes, and sensed in the blackness the shadow of evil. But these thoughts do not detain the poet for long. He plunges back into memories of how he and his friends would respond to the thrill of a storm, intoxicated by the battering of wind and wave.

And we were in a water-world
  Of rain and blizzard, sea and spray,
And one against the other hurled
  We struggled round to Greenaway.

'Trebetherick' is something more than a poem descriptive of the Cornish coast. What the coast holds for the poet is a fund of happy memories of his own childhood. The friends of those days still enrich all recollections of the scenery. Indeed it is characteristic of Betjeman as a poet that landscape in itself is rarely an exclusive interest. It tends to bring to his thoughts the people who lived with the landscape as a background. And when Betjeman reflects on a given locality which holds no special memories of acquaintances, he will sometimes people it out of his own imagination, as he does in 'Exeter' and in 'The Metropolitan Railway'.

Thus Betjeman's fullest account of the Cornish coast in this selection, 'North Coast Recollections', is a poem largely about people. The poet plants a series of little human dramas between an introduction and an epilogue which are both concerned primarily with landscape. The introduction sets the scene. It is one of quiet evening tranquillity. We see the sun setting and the house lamps being lit. A handful of little details about 'clover scent/And feathery tamarisk', 'sea-pinks', the 'silver sand', the quartz, and the twigs give immediacy to the scene. But the poet's thoughts recall how centuries of history have seen the sea rolling and thundering here. The poet returns to this vein of reflective description of the scene in the last lines of the poem.

What is sandwiched in between these opening and closing passages is a cross-section picture of the doings of various villagers on this particular evening. It is these brief sketches of village life which give the poem its vitality. There are preparations for a party at Mrs Hanks's bungalow; there is a youngsters' tournament in progress at the tennis club; there is a secret lovers' meeting between John Lambourn and Bonzo; and we see Mrs Wilder finishing her bed-time story for her youngest and then calling his two sisters in from the garden. It would be difficult to think of a poem of comparable length so packed with people, especially young people, who are vividly brought to life. Phoebe icing the cake; Gordon tinkering with the gramophone; Captain Mycroft eyeing Bonzo's charms; John Lambourn tight-throatedly lost in love for her; all these snapshots and several others stay clearly in the mind.

Betjeman does not always people his scenery. Sometimes scenery in itself can have a powerful exclusive appeal, and Cornish scenery in particular. This is evident in one of his finest poems, 'Harrow-on-the-Hill'. No external human interest intrudes here. The poet is alone with the landscape. And as he surveys the evening skyline over Harrow, the nostalgia for Cornwall is so strong that the actual scene before him is transfigured into the view over Padstow Bay.

2. Examine how the subject of death is handled in Betjeman's poetry.

Death is something of which Betjeman was acutely conscious. There are poems which take their point from the fact that death intrudes on uneventful lives. Such is 'Death in Leamington', where the poet uses the quiet death of an old lady as a fitting afternoon event in presenting the decaying gentility of the once famous Spa. Such too is 'Croydon', where the poet gives us a bird's-eye view of the way a given locality witnesses the birth, hopeful childhood, and final death of an uncle. A third instance is 'Exeter', in which a doctor rashly drives into a tram-car and is killed. In this case, it appears, the effect of bereavement upon his wife is to change her from an intellectual rebel into a faithful practising Christian. There is pathos in these poems, but no deep sense of grief. Death seems to be introduced rather for its potential in the way of narrative interest than for any urge to come to grips with grief or tragedy. Death, in short, is handled here with a detachment that precludes any sharp focus on the individual's lot.

The same may be said of the treatment of death in 'Upper Lambourne' and in 'Dorset'. The poet ponders the grave of the great trainer who had a record number of winners to his credit and then he watches horses and jockeys go off for exercise:

To the down the string of horses
  Moving out of sight and mind.

He thus offsets the immediate activities of the stable fraternity, which must be subject to death, against the unfading natural background of the downs into which they are here swallowed up. The interest in death is philosophical rather than personal. So it is in 'Dorset', where the graveyard becomes a telling, if not wholly serious, reminder that rural life must end there, and that the lives of all people, however distinguished, must end there too. Betjeman's fondness for pressing this message home is evident again at the end of 'Middlesex' with its reference to the cockney sportsmen, the Poshes and the Pooters, now 'silent under soot and stone'.

Death seems to come a little closer to the poet personally in 'The Cottage Hospital', in that he wonders what his own death-bed scene will be like, and where it will take place. But again the interest in human mortality is cerebral rather than searchingly emotional. The poet is not in pain or under any physical threat. He is lying comfortably in a garden, watching a spider trap a fly. That is what impels him to wonder about his own death. It is a matter of drawing an imaginative parallel, not a matter of trembling before the real shadow of death.

Although there is greater feeling on the subject of death in 'The Metropolitan Railway', the predominant motive for telling the story of the young couple who regularly used the line from Ruislip to the City is the desire to exploit the pathos of their lot and to see its philosophical dimensions in relation to the story of the railway they used. The death of the husband from cancer and the coming death of the wife from heart disease are not events vividly encountered in their immediacy; they are rather typical conclusions to lives which began in hope and promise. We cannot but be aware that Betjeman's prime emotional involvement is with the railway. This is not to suggest that there is any element of falsity about the poem. It is called 'The Metropolitan Railway'. Death, as a human concern, enters into the presentation in a subordinate role.

There are poems, however, where Betjeman actually gets to grips with death. The poems about his mother's death, 'Remorse', and his father's death, 'On a Portrait of a Deaf Man', are direct expressions of feelings before the spectacle of death. The physical reality is confronted in both poems without squeamishness or nicety. The moment of expiry is described in 'Remorse' in terms of rattling breath and eyes revolving in their sockets. After that, and a quick settling of the corpse by the well-trained nurse, Betjeman finds a new, inescapable train of thought. Nothing seems to matter now except his past unkindness to his mother. His father's corpse is even more gruesomely pictured in 'On a Portrait of a Deaf Man'. The contrast is sharp between the imaginative spectacle before him and the memory of the living man he knew. Suppressing any overt utterance of feeling, the poet conveys that inert blankness of inner response which the bereaved experience. The mood it stirs in him is one of bewilderment. The call to faith in God and the fact of human decay seem irreconcilable.

Oddly enough some of Betjeman's most moving poems on death seemingly spring from his own inner wells of imaginative power rather than from personal experiences of this kind. Thus 'Death of King George V' is a deeply touching poem, summing up in a few clear images not just the passing of a simple man but the passing of an age and the emergence of a threat from the future. There is no detail here of corpse or death-rattle; just the images of the closed eyes, the neglected stamp-collection, the lonely old men, and the young one who wears no hat. The quiet, oblique commentary stirs depths of pathos.

Even more touching is 'Devonshire Street W.1'. It is significant that Betjeman's most powerful poem about death is not strictly and directly about death at all. It is about the moment at which an illness is pronounced terminal. The words 'No hope' re-echo in the back of the mind. We do not see anything here so dramatic as a corpse. We see houses and the passing city crowds, a closed door and a clutch of X-ray photographs. We see a man's hand on an iron balustrade and a woman's fingers gently seeking his. We see this, and we hear talk of catching a nineteen or a twenty-two bus. That is all: yet the shock and terror of death permeate every quiet line of verse.

3. Would you agree that Betjeman's poetry shows an equal relish for the urban and the rural scene?

Betjeman was certainly not the kind of poet who draws a sharp contrast between the town and the country. There has been in English poetry a convention of contrasting the country as the background for innocence and virtue with the town as the seat of materialism and vice. It was not Betjeman's way to exploit that convention. In 'Harrow-on-the-Hill' it is the very features of the urban environment, including the noise of its traffic, that become fancifully transmuted into the landscape of his beloved Cornwall.

Betjeman does, of course, have much to say in criticism of certain urban developments. He pours scorn on the mess that the twentieth-century industrial estate has made of the old market town of Slough ('Slough'). He laments the spread of housing estates, concrete lamp-standards, and electric grids over the Hertfordshire landscape ('Hertfordshire'). Nevertheless he cannot look back upon the London suburbs of his youth without nostalgia for much that a purist nature poet would find distasteful. In 'Parliament Hill Fields' in particular he recalls his boyish delight in the trains rumbling under the 'blackened girders' of an urban railway bridge. He seems to recall with pleasure how the passing trains and trams would shake the floor and dirty the ledger in the coal merchant's office. The tram-ride home was a delight. The poet eagerly recalls the various features of the urban scene: shops, terraces, churches, and blocks of flats. There is no suggestion that the face of the earth has been despoiled by any such buildings. It is true that the young boy feels sympathy for the children whose homes lie in the more squalid parts of Kentish Town, but the contrast here is not between town and country; it is between slum and suburb.

Wordsworth felt it necessary to protest vigorously against the spread of railways into the Lake District, but in 'Essex', Betjeman's nostalgic recollection of the loved Essex of his childhood not only focuses on streams and by-roads, on thatched cottages and fifteenth-century church towers, it also romanticises

> The old Great Eastern winding slow
> To some forgotten county town.

For Betjeman it is the replacement of the railway by the motorway that is to be deplored. Indeed in 'The Metropolitan Railway' the poet sits in the buffet at Baker Street station to revel in its Victorian furnishings and to allow a reverie to develop about the kind of human story that the railway has witnessed.

It is not every poet who would be moved, by picturing the routine of daily commuting between Ruislip and the City, to visualise an imaginative parallel between the birth of a railway and the burgeoning of a love affair. As the love affair blooms, it seems to match symbolically all the human promise that was opened up on the commercial and technological side by the inception of the new electric line. Betjeman parallels the couple's tragic fate and the end of all their hopes, not with any end foreseen for the railway, but with the construction of an Odeon cinema on the site of their suburban villa. For Betjeman the clash between town and country simply does not exist in conventional terms. For him the clash is between Edwardian civilisation and the coming of the mass-production age, between the mentality that gave us railways and the mentality that has given us the Odeon cinema.

This is made evident again in 'Middlesex'. Elaine is the modern commuter who has superseded the fated couple of 'The Metropolitan Railway'. Betjeman constructs her image by listing brand-names from the fashion magazines to describe her clothes and toiletries. By the time he has told us that she settles down for the evening with sandwiches in front of the television, we have received a neat little study in the artificialities of modern life which Betjeman dislikes. For the contrasts with this study, Betjeman does not take us into rural solitude. He transports us to an idealised Victorian Middlesex which was the playground of the aspiring middle class of *The Diary of a Nobody*.

There is plenty of evidence that Betjeman relished the countryside as sensitively as he relished any urban landscape. The concise little pictures sketched in 'Essex' are alive with minutely observed detail. Remember how:

Like streams the little by-roads run
   Through oats and barley round a hill
To where blue willows catch the sun
   By some white weather-boarded mill.

The drive through Surrey in 'Love in a Valley' is pictured with the same wealth of sensitivity to flower and bush, tree and hedge, that roll by on the journey. And for sheer mastery of atmosphere in representing the rural scene perhaps there is nothing in Betjeman to surpass 'A Lincolnshire Tale'. If 'Love in a Valley' shows the countryside rapturously transfigured to the eye of love, 'A Lincolnshire Tale' shows it grimly distorted to the eye of a terrified and benighted journeyer. What is astonishing here is the speed with which the atmosphere of the countryside is transformed. Suddenly in the glimmering lights of the carriage lamps the pony drops dead, and at once images crowd upon us of awful remoteness and intense stillness; awareness looms of immense stretches of surrounding fenland invisible in the darkness.

To set this picture alongside, say, the picture of the buffet in Baker Street station ('The Metropolitan Railway') or the account of the tram-ride

from Kentish Town to Highgate ('Parliament Hill Fields') is to realise
how remarkable is Betjeman's range of sensitivity in descriptive writing,
whether of rural or urban scenes.

---

4. Consider Betjeman's qualities as a satirical poet.

One of Betjeman's most extended efforts as a satirical poet is 'The Dear
Old Village'. It sets out to contrast the accepted sentimental notion of
village life with the modern reality. The church bells, which in romantic
rural poetry generally represent the peace and charm of the village scene,
here peal out brokenly, because half the bell-ringers are on strike in dispute
over their rights to tea; and anyway the bells' call to worship is pointless
because modern people have liberated themselves from any sense of
obligation to the Creator. They would rather listen to a pop crooner than
sing hymns. Thus Betjeman introduces a survey of village life that is
corrupted by what he disapproves of – young men noisily roaring about on
their motor-bikes, and girls with painted lips and nails straddling the
pillions. Off they go to pub and cinema, ignoring the Sabbath. As for their
elders, Farmer Whistle has replaced thatched-roofed farm buildings with
concrete cowsheds; he is greedy, rich, boastful, and dishonest, he keeps a
mistress in the nearest town, and he has fathered two of Mrs Coker's
offspring. He uses his position on the Rural District Council to profiteer on
the sale of land for council-houses, having jerry-built homes erected on
undrainable terrain.

The poet's criticisms flow thick and fast. The loss of authority once
exercised by squire, parson, and schoolmaster, the closing of the village
school, transport of pupils to a town eleven miles away – in the poet's
view all these changes represent the decay of a settled, worthwhile way of
life. But the reader begins to feel a kind of mental indigestion. Betjeman's
verbal whip lashes out in too many different directions – at the modern
school curriculum, at modern school architecture, and at girls who choose
to serve in Woolworth's rather than to be housewives. On top of this
recrimination, a series of charges are made about the moral life of the
villagers, and finally about the way the men play up to sociologists doing
field-work in their local pub.

Betjeman is at best a disciplined poet, but here he allows his detestation
of mid-century developments in the environment and in social life to
rage without rein. He is more effective as a satirist when he focuses
his attack more sharply, as he does in 'Slough'. He calls there for the
obliteration of a town despoiled both in its environment and in its way
of life by the development of an industrial estate. He is more effective
still when he not only restricts his attack to a single target, but also
ceases to speak in his own voice. Thus he leaves it to the town planner
to condemn himself out of his own mouth by his boastful arrogance

in 'The Planster's Vision'. This ironic method of presentation has great advantages. As long as the poet voices his own criticism of things, as he does in 'The Dear Old Village', he runs the risk of emerging as a bad-tempered old fogey, satisfied with nothing. Making an attitude look silly through an enthusiast's defence of it gives ironic power to the critic's case.

What gives added force to the satire in 'The Planster's Vision' is that the planner is given a personality, and an unattractive one. He is arrogant and he brushes aside the interests of others. He depersonalises the villagers into mere numbers. They can be displaced without a moment's thought for what it might mean to them personally. The planner is an enthusiast, enthralled by the wonderful possibilities of a future in which a thoroughly brain-washed public inhabit a thoroughly planned environment.

Betjeman uses the same technique again in 'Executive'. The poet hits his target amusingly by condemning the executive from his own mouth:

You ask me what it is I do. Well actually, you know,
I'm partly a liaison man and partly P.R.O.
Essentially I integrate the current export drive
And basically I'm viable from ten o'clock to five.

This is funny, and satire which is funny is generally more effective than satire that is directly vituperative. Behind the voice of the executive we detect a smiling poet: in the attack on Farmer Whistle in 'The Dear Old Village' we hear an angry poet. An amusing poet is better company than an angry poet – and more persuasive, too.

The balance preserved between humour and satire varies in the poems so far considered, but in each case the target of the satire is clear. There is, however, a group of poems by Betjeman which have become widely popular and are certainly very funny, but whose satirical intent is less easy to define. The group includes 'Pot Pourri from a Surrey Garden', 'A Subaltern's Love Song', 'The Olympic Girl', and 'The Licorice Fields at Pontefract'. In these poems we are amused by the protestations of a man who aspires to the love of a strong, athletic woman and who is reduced to wilting weakness in her presence. In one of these poems, 'The Licorice Fields at Pontefract', there is a clearly definable satirical target. It plainly echoes Yeats's 'Down by the salley gardens', making fun of that kind of romantic love poetry. Instead of a nostalgic lover recalling his trysts with a gentle, delicate young maiden, we have a young man winded and wilted by the sturdy embraces of a red-haired Amazon who takes the initiative. It is thus a specimen of literary, and not social or moral, satire. In the other 'love' poems we have referred to there remains a slight element of literary satire. As is usual, the lover expresses his adoration of the beloved, but he deviates from convention by seeking to be turned to jelly in the hands of a masterful woman of immense physique. This is the kind of topsyturvydom that swamps satire in pure humour.

Part 5

Suggestions for further reading

The text

BETJEMAN, JOHN: *Collected Poems*, compiled and with an introduction by the Earl of Birkenhead, John Murray, London, 1958 (4th edition 1979, reset 1988).

Biographical works

BETJEMAN, JOHN: *Summoned by Bells*, John Murray, London, 1960. This is the poet's verse autobiography.

HILLIER, BEVIS: *Young Betjeman*, John Murray, London, 1988. The first volume of a full and detailed biography of the poet, covering the years from his birth to 1933.

——: *John Betjeman, A Life in Pictures*, John Murray in association with The Herbert Press, London, 1984. A useful and entertaining summary of the poet's life; lavishly illustrated.

THWAITES, ANN (*ed.*): *My Oxford*, Robson Books, London, 1977. A collection of reminiscences of Oxford life, including pieces by Betjeman and other public figures.

Criticism

PRESS, JOHN: *John Betjeman*, Longman, Harlow, Essex, 1974. This is a volume in the 'Writers and their Work' series.

STANFORD, DEREK: *John Betjeman, a Study*, Neville Spearman, London 1961. An early study written while Betjeman was still at work.

TAYLOR-MARTIN, PATRICK: *John Betjeman, His Life and Work*, Allen Lane, London, 1983. This is a useful guide for the student.

General background

BETJEMAN, JOHN: *Ghastly Good Taste*, Chapman & Hall, London, 1933, reprinted Anthony Blond, 1970. The sub-title of this book is 'a depressing story of the rise and fall of English Architecture'.

——: *English Cities & Small Towns*, William Collins, London, 1943. Sheds useful light on Betjeman's topographical interests: fully illustrated.

—— (with photographs by GAY, JOHN): *London's Historic Railway Stations*, John Murray, London, 1972. Sheds light on Betjeman's railway enthusiasms.

BLAMIRES, HARRY: *Twentieth-Century English Literature* (in the Macmillan History of Literature), Macmillan, London, second edition 1986. A book which puts the major writers of our century into their historic context.

Index

The index gives an alphabetical listing of the poems discussed in Part 2.

The author of these notes

HARRY BLAMIRES is a graduate of the University of Oxford, where he studied English Language and Literature. He spent a large part of his teaching life as Head of the English Department at King Alfred's College, Winchester, but retired early in 1976 to concentrate on writing. His publications include works of fiction and theology as well as literary history and criticism. He has contributed *Studying James Joyce* (1987), an introduction to Joyce's work as a whole, to the York Handbooks series, and in *The New Bloomsday Book* (Routledge 1988) he has updated his classic guide to Joyce's *Ulysses* which students have used for over twenty-five years. His *Short History of English Literature* (Methuen 1974, revised edition 1984) and his *Twentieth-Century English Literature* (Macmillan 1982, revised edition 1986), a volume in the Macmillan History of Literature (ed. A. N. Jeffares), have established his reputation as a literary historian. The present volume succeeds *The Victorian Age of Literature* (1988) and *The Age of Romantic Literature* (1990), two volumes in the York Handbooks series, and *A History of Literary Criticism* (Macmillan 1991), a further volume in the Macmillan History of Literature (ed. A. N. Jeffares).